OH WHAT A LOVELY SHORE !

Brighton in the Twenties through the eyes of a schoolboy.

by

Leonard Goldman

Published by

Leonard Goldman

26 Westfield Crescent

BRIGHTON

BN1 8JB

Printed by *digaprint*
          Unit Two
          54 Hollingdean Rd.
          Brighton BN 2 4 AA

ISBN 0 9530593 0 8

Front cover design by Tony Willard.

ACKNOWLEDGEMENTS

This book would never have been written were it not for the urging, encouragement and consistent help of Michael Hayler. He did the first editing, produced the first computerised versions and was a tower of strength in my early struggles with the computer. For all of which I am very grateful. I also have to thank Julia McGirr for her very thorough and incisive final editing - though I hasten to add that any defects of style, form or content are entirely my own. I should also like to express my thanks, firstly, to Adrian Peasegood, who kindly offered to give me a brief course in computer mechanics and, lastly, to Chris Jones for his tireless and remarkably expert assistance with the IT, without which the work could not have proceeded.

CONTENTS

INTRODUCTION

I grew up in Brighton from the age of about five and left to go to London in my sixteenth year. At that time I had no academic qualifications and little training, having left school at fourteen. Some thirty years - and a world war - later I returned as an experienced teacher to take up an appointment in a Brighton school. When I retired, fifteen years later, I was urged to write my memoirs. I resisted this suggestion for some considerable time, as I had no idea whether the general public would have the slightest interest in my story. However, the success of QueenSpark Books and their series of local autobiographies, every one of which I have read with great appreciation, convinced me that the effort might be worthwhile and that, somewhere out there, their might well be a sufficient readership to interest themselves in the story of a Brighton youth in the Twenties.

This is that story. In it, my family, friends and acquaintances are described with all the accuracy I can muster, as are my experiences, thoughts and feelings. But memory plays tricks and if there should be one who reads these lines and finds themselves referred to, or their relatives or friends or incidents of which they have personal knowledge and who wishes to correct any errors I have made, I apologise in advance and should be delighted to hear from them.

I submitted the book to QueenSpark but, for various reasons, they felt unable to publish it so I decided to put my toe in the water and see what ripples it might produce from the reading public. I have only told the story of the first fifteen-and-a-half years of my life, eleven of them in Brighton. I shall await the response with some trepidation before attempting to reveal what followed.

Note on pronunciation: In Yiddish words, ch is pronounced as in the Scottish word: loch.

For Rita, Fleur and Poppy, with love, to give

them a glimpse of what their husband, father

and grandfather was like as a boy.

ORIGINS

From the latter part of the 19th century, millions of Jews migrated westwards from eastern Europe and "Russia". They were fleeing from the bitter persecution they experienced in their ghettos, from the hostility of their neighbours, harassment from the police, brutality, murder and rapine.

Their mother tongue was Yiddish, though many also spoke Russian, Polish etc. They brought with them their vast cultural heritage and clung to the life-raft of their religion. They were not always welcomed by their co-religionists and even less by the, often unwilling, non-Jewish host population who saw them as aliens, many, indeed, as swindlers and even evil Christ-killers. But their cultural input into western society has been considerable.

My father's parents were among the early arrivals in the 1870s. My father, Myer, was born in Leeds, the first of a large family. After a short spell in America, where twin girls, Cassie and Sadie, were born, the family returned to Britain and settled down in Birmingham, in the slums of Essex Street where three more children were born, in a tiny house with an outside, shared lavatory and rather primitive facilities. My grandfather managed to eke out a livelihood as a semi-skilled cobbler in the front room of the house. I remember him as having a loud, rather coarse voice. He was a bearded man with bright red hair which soon turned grey. He was known in the community as *der gelber shooster* (the blond cobbler), .

My grandfather spoke to his family and friends in Yiddish and consequently my father spoke it fluently. He won a place at the local technical college but gave it up, perhaps because Saturday attendence breached the rules of Sabbath observance or because his earnings were required to help the family's finances.

My mother's English name was Janie, from the Russian Evgenia. Her brother called her Henya, which we children reduced to The Hen. She arrived in Britain soon after her 16th birthday. Her father was a rabbi (teacher) and she had attended the first four years at secondary school learning Russian as well as German.

My mother had been a member of the Jewish Bund, a socialist organisation banned by the Csarist authorities and this no doubt coloured her political outlook. Her mother had died early and her father took a second wife whom my mother found unsympathetic. She left and never saw her beloved father or eldest brother again, which must have been a terrible wrench.

Another brother, Yevel (Joel), for whom she worked after she got here, and sister, Esther, buxom and flirtatious and ten years her senior, were already here and established. Esther's passions were: clothes and adornment, men and food. Her marriage took her to Glasgow where her two sons were born and where she set up a dress business in the Gorbals which lasted over 50 years.

Yevel had a small business in Birmingham, where he employed my father whom he sent to meet his young sister when she arrived in England. That was the beginning of my parents' courtship; the young, shy but intelligent and determined dark-haired girl from "home" and the young man from the Birmingham ghetto, three years her senior, and thoroughly grounded in the same culture with which she had been brought up. His family, though somewhat loud and with a different ethos from her own quieter, more intellectual background, were Jewish, respectable, kind and warm and they took her to their hearts.

Her brother also had a gramophone shop in Wolverhampton, where he employed her We have a picture of her and another young lady colleague, standing outside the shop in skirts down to their ankles and wearing frilly but businesslike white blouses. He called his shop:The English Record Company because when he wanted to use his own name, Halford, it clashed with Halford's, the motor accessories people, who objected on the grounds that he would be trading under their name in "similar" goods.

Myer and Jane's courtship was pursued in the beautiful Warwickshire countryside where they went out together, on bicycles or a tandem. They often described these outings to us, later, when we were old enough to understand. But they seem to have given up cycling when they got married.

His business consisted of enlarging and framing customers' own pictures, which door-to-door canvassers had previously obtained from them. We have a wonderful set of magnificent Edwardian picture postcards, of special interest to us because, on the back, they carry their correspondence in the years before their marriage, 1910 and 1911. The picture of my father which they reveal is fascinating. They chronicle his travels from place to place, seeking business in a dozen different towns from the Midlands to the South. His various business activities and problems were the main topics he touches on.

He also gives details of his lodgings and, sometimes, a word or two about the town, itself. However, he always ends with "fondest love" or "love and kisses", which are an indication of how far their courtship had progressed and I suppose my mother had to be content with that as an indication of his romantic feelings! The cards she sent to him are mainly expressions of concern for his welfare.

They married in 1912. She was in traditional white (amazing how little bridal gowns have changed in 80 years!) and he in full morning dress. By that time he had a small menswear shop in the Gorbals area of Glasgow, having temporarily given up the picture business, which Yevel had taught him.

They were married in 1912.

On their way home from their honeymoon, my father announced that the business was failing. However, they hung on long enough for my two elder sisters, Helen and Gertrude ("Gertie") to be born in the small "but-and-ben" (two-roomed house) as well as to conceive their only son. But I am not a Scotsman, as they moved to Stourport in Worcester, where I was born on August 7th 1916. It was Bank Holiday Monday and the bells were ringing and my mother felt it was some kind of omen.

"The Great War" had been going on for two years and my father was called up to the Royal Garrison Artillery. He eventually went to France. On his way to the boat he popped in to see mother, a visit that resulted in the birth of another daughter, Etta, in Bournemouth, where his sister, Cassie, (one of the twins born in America) was also living. Mother loved seasides and Bournemouth was to be the first of three in which we lived.

Whilst in France, my father got a "Blighty one" - a slight wound that got him sent home, the dream of every soldier serving abroad. Carrying a heavy shell across icy ground, he slipped and fell. The shell must have pressed on his little finger and he bore the wound, a slightly squashed little finger, until his dying day.

At home, he was stationed at Rippon, in Yorkshire and used to cycle from the camp to the nearby cottage where the family (now four children) were in lodgings. One of my earliest memories was of a large cycle in the hall. On his demobilisation, we all moved to Weston-Super-Mare, on the Bristol Channel

It was here that we first became acquainted with Auntie Esther and my Scottish cousins, Harold and Arnold, with their exotic accent. It was from them that I learnt my first swearwords and "the facts of life", all in heavy Glaswegian. They were my replacement elder brothers.

We also met Mr. and Mrs. Rudy in Weston and their three children, Donya, Sara and Wolfie, the youngest, who was six months older then me. Both parents were Russian immigrants, like my mother. His first wife had died very young, when Donya and Sara were small and his second wife was her elder sister who came over from Russia to look after the two girls. They married and she produced a son, Wolfie, who was the apple of their eye.

They both spoke Russian, especially when talking to each other and to my mother, and their children also picked up a smattering of it. Their mother tongue was Yiddish and my father could converse with them in that. They spoke a heavily accented English. It is, perhaps, interesting to note that, although they soon became our fast friends, they and my parents always addressed each other as, Mr. and Mrs., and never used first names. Mr. R.'s hypersensitivity made him highly nervous and irascible, given to bursts of anger. He was also very musical though with no training. He read a lot, mainly in Russian.

His wife was less educated but very astute and he greatly valued her practical capabilities, common sense and stoicism. Donya learnt the violin and, when she went to live in London with an aunt, she attained a certificate in the instrument. Sara was a tomboy with little liking for serious things. She was full of life and giggled a lot and sometimes aroused her father's ire.

Wolfie showed remarkable ability at an early age. Already literate before he went to school, for which his father must take some credit, he was interested in everything, a faculty which has certainly stood him in good stead and advanced his academic progress. He started school in Weston and was immediately outstanding. He has, subsequently, had a history of academic success. We became inseparable friends. His influence was in many ways greater than that of my cousins.

The earliest family photograph, ca 1918.

From as far back as I can remember, our family always had a maid, usually a country girl looking for work in service. Our first in Weston-super-Mare was Nellie, who became part of the family. It was my eldest sister, however, who had the task of being a little mother to the other children. She was in charge and had ways of seeing that we did not step out of line. Pinching was one of her disciplinary methods. She also cleverly invented a quite unique kind of game to make us good . We had to sit absolutely still and "think good thoughts". The impossibly virtuous feeling this engendered is one I can recall with great clarity.

Our house was situated near Grove Park. This was one of our main playgrounds. There was an open entrance leading into a beautiful flower garden. I was overtopped by some of the tall flowers and when I entered I felt shut in, in a mysterious and scented world. The perfume was overpowering, bringing a feeling of awe and even a little fear that comes floating back to me over the years, still intense and vivid whenever I smell the powerful scent of masses of fresh geraniums. By the time I reached the open field beyond, my mood had changed as I headed for the lone bandstand. The seemingly vast stretch of grass brought the desire to run wild, to lie on my back gazing at the sky, to feel free - but also lonely - and to look for playmates.

Near the entrance was an open air stage on which concert parties would sometimes perform. On one occasion, my cousin, Arnold, climbed a fence-post from which he got a good view of the stage, with the intention of taking part in the performance. He had a supply of small paper bags which he blew into, filled with air and closed at the top by twisting, effectively creating paper balloons. A young lady sang a song that went;

Pop in and see pretty Poppy one day
At the pop, the pop, the lollipop shop.

At each pop, my cousin banged one of the bags to make it go pop in time with the song. It didn't create much of a stir but we both enjoyed it hugely.

At the other end of the field, the park rose quite steeply towards a dark wooded area. We played many games there, involving hiding and fighting and whispering our childish secrets, hopes and fears, away from adult eyes, where we could indulge our imagination, so quickly lost in adult life.

I also remember the extensive sandy beaches where, although we couldn't swim, we went in bathing at low tide when the sea went out and you had a long walk over an enormous stretch of muddy flat sand, just to paddle. There were rocks along one end of the front, covered with seaweed and many a grazed limb we had climbing their slippery surfaces. There were a few loose stones and I once filled my cap with them and, using it as a kind of sling, attempted to cast the stones into the water. Naturally, the hat went in, too. I tried it again a few weeks later - with the same result, despite my eldest sister's watchful eye. This time I got into serious trouble and was effectively cured of such pranks.

Sometimes we went walking in the countryside with the Rudys. There was a wood, not far from the town, which was one of our favourite destinations. We also often walked to Uphill, a few miles south of Weston. On one such occasion, Harry Gold, a distant relative who later became a close friend of the family and who was a bit of a daredevil, came with us. We saw a horse, looking over a hedge and he gave it an apple. When it opened its mouth for more, he thrust his hand right inside and calmly scraped the frothy, white saliva from the top of its tongue. Ugh! I thought about the slime all through supper.

It was whilst we were still in Weston that I must have shown some early precocity. My mother used to tell the story of how she found me deep in conversation with an elderly man on a park bench. He remarked on the maturity of my arguments. I hesitate to suggest that at that early age I was already developing that pugnacious and passionately argued political stance that I adopted later in life. I do remember, however, that I liked to argue, even as a child. My acquaintances will tell you that it has got worse with age.

Another memory of Weston is of an old game, from which the expression: putting up your own Aunt Sally, is derived. It was in an arcade near the front, that I saw one of these Aunt Sally stalls. It was a bit like a coconut shy; the thrower stood at a bar and was given three wooden balls. At a distance of about six to eight feet, there was a door with a large black spot as a target, right in the middle of it.

If you hit the spot, the door opened and a life-sized, wooden figure of a woman rolled slowly down a slope towards you, on metal rails. This was the Aunt Sally that has come down to us in the form of a metaphor. I don't know if such a game still exists, but the political "game" of putting up your own Aunt Sally certainly does!

It was in Weston that my father again started up in the business to which Yevel had introduced him, the picture business, which was to be his sole source of livelihood for the rest of his working life. The canvasser obtains a photograph, promising to bring it back with an enlargement for which no charge is made and without any obligation to purchase. But the aim is to persuade her (inevitably it was a housewife) to have the enlargement "finished" or coloured and framed.

My father employed canvassers to obtain the pictures but he called back himself, with the "proofs", to try and "pass" them, i.e to get an order. A firm in London, Barlow's, serviced the burgeoning number of such businesses by producing cheap enlargments of about 12"x18". They also did the framing. From a studio portrait the result might be very good. But the seaside snaps, when enlarged, were often hardly recognisable. In the post-war period, with many having lost husbands and sons, business was good. Once touched up or coloured and framed, the pictures were sometimes excellent and the customer was getting a worthwhile article, though probably at an inflated price.

The framed pictures were quite heavy and my father employed a carrier, with pony and trap, to ferry him round on his deliveries. He had a woman artist in Devon, a Miss Solomons, to whom he sent the orders for colouring and who was quite a competent artist.

THE BRIGHTON SAGA BEGINS

About 1920 or '21, we left Weston for Brighton. Maybe Weston was too far from the centre of things and Brighton seemed a better area for business; and it was a seaside. On the journey to Brighton my father pointed out to us the famous White Horse, carved in chalk on a hill in Wiltshire, as we flashed passed it. My younger sister, Etta, recalls that she had been instructed to sit in a kind of kneeling position, with her feet tucked under her, so as to look more babyish and justify the cheaper fare they had paid for her !

Much later, my mother told me that her friends had warned her that Brighton was a wicked place, with dangerous predatory women waiting to husband-snatch. Brighton's naughty image was something that only impinged on my consciousness as I grew older. But, right from the beginning, there was a certain feeling of fresh breezes blowing, of an atmosphere at once modern, libertarian, and full of possibilities.

Along the front we saw the pebbly beach, so very different from the sandy shore we knew; the two piers, resplendent in what seemed like permanent sunshine; the great Metropole and Grand Hotels, standing like symbols of an impossible affluence, of another world that we would never inhabit. Then there were the "charabangs" (as we pronounced it) touting for custom and promising heavenly outings to Sussex beauty spots.

Our first abode was a basement flat at 40 Russell Square, near the little passageway leading to Regency Square. At the beginning of the passageway was a little dairy, whose window display impressed my child's mind. During our short stay there, we were visited by my Uncle Harry, a visit that was to be the first of a veritable stream of visits from uncles, aunts and cousins from both sides of the family. A seaside is a great attraction!

We soon moved to No.5 Powis Square, which was to be our permanent home for the rest of our ten-year stay in Brighton. It was a three-storey building (four if you count the basement). It must have been comparatively expensive, probably about a thousand pounds (over a hundred-thousand at today's prices). It is still standing and looking outwardly much the same as it did then,although it has now been dvided into several self-contained flats. Clearly business had been good during the Weston days, so we were, at that stage, fairly prosperous.

The basement was already occupied by tenants, a middle-aged Irish couple, the Landons. They were the sweetest couple you could wish to meet who often invited me downstairs for a cup of tea, when we had quite serious and lengthy discussions. They had an Irish terrier called Susie. It was rather dark down there but the gloom was lightened by their smiling faces. Their accent was delicious.

The doorway to the house was, and still is, rather imposing. The front steps, covered in small, square, white tiles, with black diamond squares at each corner, led to a heavy door with a brass knocker. Inside there was quite a longish hall leading to the staircase. Although there were two large rooms downstairs, we usually ate in the fairly large kitchen. The cooking and washing facilities were in a small extension. Even in a house like this, there was no running hot water. All water for washing etc. downstairs had to be boiled.

From the scullery there was a door to the backyard, a small cemented area surrounded by a narrow border of earth. We kept the dustbin out there and the dustmen had to traipse right through the house and the kitchen (where there might be washing hanging on a pulley to dry!) in order to get to the bin and they carried it high on their back. Mother used to wash our hair in a zinc bath in the scullery. From the yard we could look down, over protecting railings, into the Landons' yard down below.

Upstairs there was the bathroom, where hot water was obtained from a gas-fired geyser which filled the bath very slowly. Lodgers were charged sixpence (2 1/2p) per bath to cover the cost of the gas. Our family's bedrooms were also on this floor. The front bedroom had a balcony overlooking the square. The second and third floor rooms were let to tenants. I can, for instance, remember a Jewish family, the Phillips', on the second floor. They had one daughter. He had a barber's shop in town and seemed quite prosperous.

The daughter was a girl in her middle teens who was learning hairdressing. In those days gents' and ladies' saloons were usually quite separate. She was also learning the piano and we heard her thumping away at her exercises. It may have been this which persuaded my mother to have us taught.

We were quite friendly with them and once, when my parents went to Ascot, they entertained us with a lovely meal of fried fish. I noticed how different their cooking was to ours. What sticks in my mind was that the fish was somehow larger and the method of frying similar to that in a fish and chip shop. During the day Mr. Phillips took me on a steamer trip. We boarded the ship from the West Pier landing stage and cruised along the coast. The steamship company advertised outside his shop and he got free tickets for the boat. We ate a banana each during the trip, and I felt a bit queasy.

When we moved into the house, we bought a whole houseful of new furniture and fittings.   We had some heavy, highly polished mock 18th century pieces: sideboard, wardrobe and dressing table, with impressive inlaid border designs. The main double-bed matched them, too. All beds were of the spring-based frame type with head-boards top and bottom and stuffed horse-hair matresses; divan beds were unheard of. A large table, which could be expanded (and on which I later played my first table tennis) stood in the front room together with six very imposing, solid chairs with padded seats covered in shining leatherette.   In the next room, a gate-leg drop-flap oval table was opened out for meals.

My father's lack of do-it-yourself skills meant that he always had to be on the lookout for some local craftsman to do the necessary household repairs and decoration.   Not long after we moved to Powis Square, he was introduced to a painter and decorator, a Mr. Clements, who from that time on was always called upon to carry out the practical jobs that arose from time to time and he became our adviser and confidant.

The little garden in the middle of the square was surrounded by an iron-railed fence.   There were two locked gates and only residents had keys. We children used it a lot as a playground. Our parents were happy that we were safe and secure there. But some of the older inhabitants were less happy.   The "Old Geysers", Arnold once christened them, and old geysers they remained for ever afterwards.   One old lady, in particular, who lived at number 10, near the top of the square, used to look out of her ground-floor window, resting on her elbows, balefully staring at us and pouring out a stream of testy complaints.

There were few other children resident in the square but one family, the Cartwrights, had two, Brenda, of our own age and Thomas, somewhat older who attended Brighton College.   The father was head of the prosperous estate agents who, I believe, are still in existence.   Tommy was a large boy (his sister was quite plump, too) and loved cricket. They lived at No. 12 and we were invited round to their house occasionally to play a kind of cricket in their tiny garden. It wasn't real cricket but it was fun.   We also enjoyed the generous provision of home-made lemonade and biscuits served up by his mother, a tiny woman by comparison with her children, who evidently resembled the father.

It was Tommy who introduced me to smoking - Dr.Blosser's herbal cigarettes for asthma sufferers - and who told his little sister, when she was reluctant to let us ride on her fairy-bicycle, "Now remember, they are the only little playmates you have round here."

The grocer's in our local shopping area was owned by a Mr.

Trethowen (a Cornishman) whose son went to my school. Diagonally across the road from them was a dairy. There is a car workshop there now. This dairy had butter displayed in the window with beautiful pictures stamped on it. The milk was served out in a metal ladle with a long handle and a mug-shaped scoop holding half a pint, which was emptied into the customer's own receptacle. Milk was not delivered to the door in a bottle.

The Seven Dials was within walking distance. It was a tram junction and swooping down New England Hill on a tram was one of the thrills I shall never forget. There was always a large policeman known as Fatty Arbuckle, directing the traffic at the top. It was rumoured that he later committed suicide. We youngsters called this "suet pudden", blissfully unaware of the tragedy that lay behind it.

We could see St. Michael's Church from our house, a landmark in those days as it is today. I only knew it from outside but I often spent weary hours waiting for some of my friends to come out of Sunday School from the side entrance. For obvious reasons, I did not attend Sunday School, myself. The first time I saw the interior was a few years ago, when a colleague was married there.

We regarded Montpelier St. as "our hill". Whether we toiled up it on a hot day, sweating and puffing, or struggled up it, wet and shivering and cold in rainy weather, it was always familiar territory. We had friends who lived there and we often stopped for a chat on the way. One of the worst tasks was dragging our heavy beach tent up and down - usually my job - until we got wise (or less parsimonious) and parked it in one of Jim Hatton's beach huts for what now seems a tiny sum.

Sometimes my father would propel one of us up by planting the tip of his walking stick in the small of the back and gently applying pressure, all the way to the top. I'm not sure whether the discomfort in the spine was worth it. There were few cars in those days and only the relatively wealthy could afford a taxi, so it was a main pedestrian thoroughfare for all our neighbours. I seldom used it as a route to and from school but, in addition to journeys to the beach, it became a regular daily walk as soon as I started work.

At the top of Montpelier St. and on the corner of Victoria Rd. there was a sweet shop where I first spent the odd pennies I managed to accumulate, mainly on icecream, at a penny a small cornet. Later, however, the father of one of my schoolfriends converted his home, on the diagonally opposite corner, into a sweetshop, too. The story was that he had a grudge against the other chap because of some unspecified dirty trick he was supposed to have played on his wife who, incidentally, was French. After that, woe betide any of us who dared to patronise the other shop!

THE FAMILY AND OTHER INFLUENCES

By present day standards, we were a largish family, six in all. There were Helen, Gertie, myself and Etta, in order of appearance. My parents were very different in character, temperament, talents and perceived needs. But their common background, shared experiences and problems tackled, their love of their children and their own strong mutual affection bound them together.

My father was quick at figures and, although he was not interested in serious literature, had a rather jocular affection for wordplay and simple crosswords and was good at cards - especially solo. He did not read many books, though quite late in life, he could still recite poems he had learnt by heart, at school. Once, when he was already quite elderly, he suddenly, and without warning, recited a German poem to me, which he had learnt as a boy. He occasionally recited English poems, too, in a ringing, singing voice. But here I must mention that he was quite tone deaf. I always put down my own inability to hold a tune to this deficiency of his. One other thing he taught me was the mnemonic for the colours of the rainbow, ROYGBIV, which I still use.

He used many phrases and expressions that he had picked up in the army, in World War One. For rain he'd say "parni" (from pani, Hindustani for water), or "bevvy", for drink (perhaps from beverage?). He also used backslang: "Ighmey bly" for Blimey and he'd take us through a whole sentence in similar vein. I can still hear it in his Birmingham accent. He had also acquired a whole vocabulary in Cockney rhyming slang. A hat was always a "titfer" (tit-for-tat).and he called trousers, "strides"; Birmingham slang, perhaps.

He had brought with him from the army and, even further back, from the Edwardian music hall days of his youth, a number of popular songs of the day. And it was from his rendering(!) of these that I first learnt them, myself. *It's a long way to Tipperary, There's a long, long lane a'winding, till my dreams all come true, Keep the home fires burning* (a sentimental song that bound the troops at the front to their loved ones at home) and *Bluebell* (about a girl he had left at home - "*Mid camp fires gleaming, Mid shot and shell, and all the while I'm dreaming of my own Bluebell*").

I've heard these songs sung many times since, even attempted to sing them myself, and thoroughly enjoyed some of them in, for instance, *Oh, what a lovely war!* But almost always my mind goes back to my Dad, belting them out in his tuneless voice; for me, still the authentic rendering! Life dealt him a number of hard knocks but he had relatively simple tastes and he never lost his boyish love of tricks, harmless jokes and recounting stories of his youth. A good meal and jolly company, with his family around him, could always put him in a good mood.

On dull days at home, he played many card games with us: whist, German whist, patience (solitaire) and solo, which he also played more seriously with his friends. Ludo was another board game we played. Great was the excitement as our coloured buttons chased each other round the board to "home".

My father had agreed to come to Brighton, prompted by my mother, who was determined to live at the seaside, as she was convinced that this was "healthier" and health was her watchword. Weston was a seaside, too, but business was beginning to dry up there, as it was becoming a kind of backwater and he believed that, as there was more going on in Brighton, prospects for his business would be better.

He was prepared to work hard and could certainly sweet-talk the customers. His business took him to other areas, from time to time, but he was always back home in the evening. In his younger years, he was a heavy smoker, 20 to 30 cigarettes a day. However, from time to time he suffered from quinzy, an inflammation of the throat. When that happened, the doctor always advised him to stop smoking until it got better, which usually took a couple of weeks. After several bouts of this illness, he decided to try and prolong the non-smoking period.

He did this so successfully that he never smoked again. Now this happened at a vital moment for me, when many of my pals were experimenting with cigarettes and often gave me a puff, usually on walks over the Downs. But as there were never any at home, I never became addicted and have remained a life-long non-smoker.

I also remember going down with my father to the fish market on a Sunday morning. I don't think Fishermen's Hard had been built at that time but the boats were all drawn up on the beach in that area and fresh fish (just caught in many cases) was sold at knockdown prices, direct from the side of the boats. The little boys who helped the fishermen were often given a netful of herrings as "wages", which they sold at something like 12 for a shilling!

Father was increasingly worried about the business and was sometimes too tired, preoccupied or irritable to give us the attention we demanded. However, when things were going well, he would take us out for a re-fitting, shoes, trousers etc. or treat us to an icecream or a charabanc ride, or a ride on Volk's Electric Railway: he was basically a very kind-hearted man.

One spin-off from my father's cigarette smoking was the supply of cigarette cards that it engendered. Most cigarette packets had cards inside them as a form of sales promotion. The subjects covered were many and varied. One I remember was devoted to famous cricketers. On the reverse was a detailed description of the player and his career to date. The tobacco company, Carreras, produced a cigarette called Black Cat. Their cards had coloured designs on them. When the collection was complete, these could be sewn onto a black velvert cushion which they provided if you collected a set. What a great pity I didn't realise the value that these collections would accrue.

My father was never very fashionably dressed, an inch or so of sock always showing beneath his trousers. Arnold once remarked, in his braw Glaswegian accent: "Uncle Myer's trousers don't speak to his shoes." He was no great gambler but he did like his little bet on the horses, especially during Brighton races though we never actually went to the race-course. There was an incident, in this connection, which he repeatedly recounted.

It appears that he had backed a horse with his bookie, a certain Mr. Black. The horse lost. But when my father 'phoned to raise a query on another matter, Mr. Black immediately said: "That's OK Mr. Goldman, we know you intended to back X (the winner) and we're sending you the cheque through the post." "What a gentleman he was !", my father often remarked.

I don't believe my father was seriously religious but until well into middle age he maintained the forms. Though he gradually stopped attending synagogue on the Sabbath, we always celebrated the main Jewish festivals and fasted on *Yom Kippur* (Day of Atonement). One advantage was that we children got these as extra holidays from school.

It was and still is the practice in many Jewish homes for the children - and especially the boys - to learn Hebrew, so that they could pray in that language. Boys have to recite or sing(!) a portion of the law in synagogue, before the whole congregation, on or around their thirteenth birthday, on their Barmitzvah, something like Confirmation.

There are other festivals, some involving rituals at home, where ability to pray in Hebrew is essential. Of course, it is expected that you will actually understand what you are reading and some people undoubtedly do, perhaps the majority these days, but at least the ability to read the words, i.e. master the alphabet, was a minimum requirement.

Hebrew has no letters representing vowels, which are only indicated by small diacritical marks below the letters. I learnt the alphabet and can still read Hebrew, after a style, though I'm out of practice now. Our teacher was Mrs. Stein, a large foreign lady and when, in trying some elementary visual aid she said, slowly, *pahneem*, (face) and circled her own face with her index finger, the process took quite a while!

Later my instruction both in the language and the ritual performance was taken over by the rabbi at the Synagogue. I found myself with a small coterie of other boys, sitting in the hall at the back and coming under a much more disciplined form of learning. Here it was that I discovered that I should have to read from the scroll of law, removed from the ark every *Shabbas* (Sabbath), the portion that was due to be read on that particular Saturday.

The Hebrew on that scroll was not written with the vowel marks, as in the usual prayer book, but without them, another hazard to add to my imperfect knowledge of the language and my lack of fluency in reading it. The contrast between my mastery of English, both reading and writing, for which I was already one of the more advanced at school, and my inabilities in Hebrew, was particularly embarrassing to me.

I had heard stories of other boys who had confidence, sang their "portion" musically and afterwards came over to their admiring families and kissed their mother, who was glowing with pride. I hardly think that my Barmitzvah performance came up to that standard. I have never been backward in public when I have been confident in what I was saying or doing. In this case I was neither. I think I stumbled through the ordeal with minimal competence and, instead of feeling that I had entered the Jewish community as a paid up member, felt more alienated than ever.

We had a very enjoyable family gathering at home, however, and I received gifts from one and all, including the traditional fountain-pen. I also got: *The History of the Jews in England* from Harry Gold and the *Chumash* (The Old Testament) in English and Hebrew. His mother gave me an English edition of the Talmud. According to the introduction, it is "...... an encyclopaedia of law, civil and penal, human and divine.....of a thousand years of the national life of the Jewish people....oral traditions......standard study.....endeared to the people."

The book lies before me now on my desk and I cannot resist the temptation to quote her inscription in full:

"In remembrance of your Barmitzvah. I trust you will grow

up to be a good and true Jew, to live up to the teachings of your people and remain a credit to your parents as well as to the Jewish comunity (her spelling). Yours lovingly, Mrs. Hanah Gold"

. Harry became an emotionally committed Zionist in later life and I had many a political battle with him, some quite acrimonious. I have been affected by my Jewish origins in many different ways. But I have always recoiled from the warm embrace of the "community" with its religious, social and, in post-war times, nationalistic implications.

On *Erev Shabbas* (Sabbath Eve)that is on Friday night, when the Sabbath begins, my mother used to bless the lights. Two candles were lit, in long brass candlesticks, and placed at the head of the table. There was a bright, white tablecloth and everything looked clean and inviting. In front of the candles was a large dish with a huge *chola* (white plaited bread) on it. Mother performed the ritual before my father came home. She would make a little forward, circular movement with her hands, cover her eyes gently with her fingers and recite a few words of prayer. These Sabbath rites remain crystal clear in my mind.

At *Pesach* (Feast of the Passover) there were also ceremonies at home. All *Chometz* (anything connected with bread) had to be hidden away and only Matzo (unleavened bread) eaten. There was even special crockery and cutlery used for the purpose. But there was a ceremony, too. All Jewish festivals begin at night, when the sun goes down. And the first night of *Pesach* is *Seder* Night. This is celebrated with a meal and special prayers.

There is a special prayer book for this called the *Hagaddah*, which lays down the order of events. Special foods are eaten and everyone is supposed to relax, sitting at ease, to remind us of the exodus from Egypt and how God delivered us from slavery. We eat bitter herbs as a reminder of our sufferings and sit at ease to remind us of our delivery from "bondage" - a word much loved by the translators.

The highlight of the evening is the asking of the *Feer Kashas* (four questions) by the youngest son (or daughter, if there are no sons), from the *Hagaddah*. The opening words are printed on my mind, both the Hebrew and the English translation:

The boy begins by asking the key question: "Wherefore is this night distinguished from all other nights?". The questions continue, referring to all the differences in food, manner of sitting and so on. The father replies to each question in turn, explaining that this is a commemoration of the escape from slavery and the gratitude we should show to the Almighty- "Blessed be He" (the obligatory exclamation after any mention of His name).

There are rules governing food, too; important dietary laws which are part of Jewish tradition. These relate to certain foods which are forbidden altogether, such as any pig products, game or shellfish. Apart from this, all meat has to be slaughtered according to the method laid down. The reader may have seen signs outside "Kosher" butcher's shops. The term proclaims that their meat has been killed by the permitted method. At that time even Jews like my father, who were not fanatically religious, tended to patronise these shops. It may have been just habit, group conformity or even a feeling that Kosher meat was somehow cleaner.

The shop we dealt with was in Waterloo St. The visits there also gave my mother the opportunity to catch up on community gossip. These places were seen as something of a marriage market. The market could best be tested in shops where other members of the community foregathered. Incidentally, marriage outside the community is strictly forbidden in Jewish law. Marrying a *Shiksa* or *Shaygitz* (non-Jewish boy or girl) was considered a scandal in those days.

There were times when the strains imposed by financial difficulties caused domestic rifts and even rows and I know mother was sometimes sad about our problems and the resultant emotional disturbance they caused. Nonetheless, the overall impression I retain in my mind is of family harmony and happily united parents.

My mother's mastery of English was the envy of all our Yiddish-speaking friends but as she improved her English, she gradually lost fluency in Russian and even, to some extent, in Yiddish, her mother tongue. Her English was elegant though she did retain a slight foreign accent and many English people judged her to be Scottish or from the North. Her early days in Birmingham also left some trace of a Midlands accent.

She was an intensely emotional woman whose whole being was centred around the family and especially the children. Our friends regarded her as something of a fanatic when it came to matters of health, particularly healthy eating. Fruit was almost an obsession with her.

She had read *Nature's Way* by Reddie Mallett, who advocated pip-water as beneficial so, in addition to eating oranges and drinking fresh orange juice, we also had to drink the water in which the pips had been soaked. It was almost tasteless and quite unpleasant. The only sweets she really approved of were Fox's Glacier Mints and her handbag always contained a supply of these, usually horribly stuck together.

Her real idol was Sir William Arbuthnot Lane, "Arbie" in my father's joking parlance. He was a pioneer of healthy eating and I believe it was he who coined the phrase:"You dig your grave with your teeth!" An abundance of fresh fruit and green vegetables are now recognised as vital sources of vitamins, (she pronounced it "vite-a-mines") iron etc. without which the body rapidly deteriorates. But in those days it was regarded, at best, as an eccentricity, at worst as an obsession.

After we had started school we always took either an apple or a banana with us to eat during "playtime". We also only had wholemeal bread as advocated in *Nature's Way*, not white *qvatch* (rubbish) as she scornfully called it. She was not exactly a hyperchondriac but health was her priority and she was very strict about our eating habits. Indeed, she made quite a fetish of it. We had to clear the plate or there was trouble. I can still see her thick little strong, capable fingers pressing down forcefully on the orange, draped over the squeezer, as it yielded every drop of its juice. Which reminds me of a lovely little verse, composed by my sister, Helen, when she was "into" poetry. It was called, *Janie*, and started, *Little fat fingers clutch the glass, Every ounce of juice must come.*

Mother also examined us visually for any signs which she might interpret as of lowered physical standards or performance, like a pale complexion or tiredness. We were all a pretty healthy bunch and I think I was quite robust, but my mother was firmly convinced that I had thyroid deficiency.

She must have got the idea once, when she took me to the doctor for some real or imaginary ailment and perhaps he had suggested it to her. From that time onwards, I had to take thyroid pills, which were very expensive - and that at a time of financial difficulty! Insistence on a healthy way of life is not a bad principle - as long as you don't exaggerate it for, as we know in other spheres, it can then turn into its opposite. My eldest sister was kept away from school for long periods because mother decided she was not well enough to attend.

At one point, I was admitted to hospital for observation. Thus I became acquainted with the Royal Sussex County Hospital for the first (but alas not the last) time. It was quite an adventure, especially as I wasn't really ill. I hated the inactivity and when I could see, through the ward windows, some men playing football, I wanted to join in. I remember dashing round the ward, in my rather loose slippers, and kicking an imaginary ball.

One slipper went flying off into the air and landed on the bed of an old boy, probably much younger than I am now, who didn't appreciate it at all. I was discharged after a few days when they found there was nothing wrong with me. In later life, my mother was given to boasting that she had laid down a healthy way of life for us in childhood

One very real source of health worry, however, was her bronchitis. She got it every year and had to have special medicine which did not seem to be all that effective. During these bouts, her condition produced a gloomy atmosphere in the house. But, just as quickly as she had contracted it, when the season changed it disappeared. In later life it left her altogether.

She had an avid interest in literature throughout her life. Indeed, she attained a very high level of competence in English, partly through her extensive reading especially of Dickens, her first favourite. She once told me that her English-born sisters-in-law got her to write their letters for them, as her style and command of terminology was superior to theirs.

The books she preferred were stories of frustrated love, as long as they also had literary merit. One was *If Winter Comes*, by H.S.M. Hutchinson and another was *Rogue Herries*, by Hugh Walpole. Both stories were superbly recounted to me by my mother who related them bit by bit, as she read them. I can still hear the catch in her voice as, eaten up by the pathos, she came to the sad parts, still see the hint of tears when relating moments of particular kindness or unexpected joy and good fortune as she became quite choked with emotion. She was deeply affected by someone's kindness or self-sacrifice.

Always striving for spiritual and cultural improvement, my mother decided that we should all learn the piano. None of us was musically gifted, quite the contrary, but Myer acquiesced as he usually did in the end and we were all enrolled with a Miss Singer, who came to the house once a week to teach us on the upright piano which was specially bought for the purpose.

Miss Singer was a petite young lady, with a very pale face, a remarkable nose, heavily carmined lips and long, bright red and highly polished finger nails. None of us practised as regularly as we were supposed to. Helen, ever the rebel, dropped out after a short resistance which we others could not match.

I did make a certain limited progress, myself. It was strangely calming to thump out the simplified versions of well known pieces, which was the teacher's approach to motivation.   Such bowdlerised versions of classical or "serious" music are frowned upon by the experts these days, no doubt rightly.   But I still remember the melodies we played and - despite my musical deafness - recognised them when I heard them played in their original form, many years later.

One effect of having a piano was that it was possible for friends who could really play to entertain us when they came to visit, as one schoolfriend, Ernie Bale did.   Apart from playing for us at times, he tried to let me in to the secrets of the world of music.   Our piano lessons soon ceased, however, partly because of waning interest and the dawning appreciation by my mother that we were not very musically gifted and partly, no doubt, for financial reasons.

There are two other things I remember about my mother.   The only cosmetic she ever used was Pond's vanishing cream.   Whenever I am aware of its use on other women I am instantly reminded of her putting me to bed when I was very young or bending forward washing my knees when I was a little older.   She was also very addicted to Henry Heath hats, when she could afford them - which wasn't very often.

In contrast to my father, who was tone deaf, she had a sweet melodious voice, at least so it seemed to me on the very rare occasions when she might suddenly break into a Russian song.   Her singing voice was so unlike her speaking voice that it sounded quite eerie.   I can well remember the peculiar feeling it induced in me, as though she were someone else, a stranger, inhabited by a strange spirit.   Her sister, Esther, had a feel for music, sang a lot, as did her two sons, both of whom could play the piano by ear.

Mother was a master of good, traditional Jewish cooking.   Her chicken and roast potatoes were always delicious as was the chicken soup and *loksh'n* (noodles), which she prepared herself, from a mixture of flour and eggs, and cut into long strips, which were then cooked in the soup. The other traditional soup filling was *knaydlach* (feather-light dumplings, made with matzo-meal).   She was well known in our circles for these dishes.

My father's favourite dish, which I also devoured with relish, was *tsim'ss*: chopped carrots fried in chicken fat, delicious! Cholosterel?   We'd never heard of it.   She also made what we called *blintsers*, a mixture of grated raw potatoes and egg, made into a ball, flattened, then fried in oil.   But she also showed her versatility in these matters, by learning English-style cooking, too.   The only traditional dish she never seemed to make was Yorkshire pudding.

Everything else was grist to her mill: roast beef and roast

potatoes or steak and onions with chips or mashed potatoes at which she was particularly good. She even learnt how to make Christmas pudding and mince pies. We were, however, not so keen on her insistence on cabbage and spinach, which we disliked. For some reason I was not keen on her baked apples or rice pudding either, both of which I learnt to enjoy in later life

Her, brother, Uncle Yevel, was a nut-brown little man with a shining bronzed scalp and intense brown eyes. His mind always seemed to be elsewhere when you spoke to him. He had the wondering look of a lost child. He visited us regularly in Brighton and he was always full of new schemes. One was a project for the manufacture of a special new face cream. He got as far as inventing a name, "Lemondu" - it was going to be lemon-scented - designing the little jar which was to contain the preparation and roughing out an advertisement for it. It was to feature a young lady, with the open jar in one hand, applying the cream to her face with the other. The model he used was my sister, Helen. She looked very fetching. But sadly, as with his numerous other schemes, this photograph is all that remains of the great plans he had for producing and marketing the stuff.

Uncle Yevel also became a competition addict. Having picked the *least* likely solution, he was not only convinced that it was the best, but that his genius would be recognised in some suitable way. Week followed week and when he heard nothing he would say - quite seriously, for he had no sense of humour, "They are pondering over my entry. They can't understand how anyone was able to see through them." Somewhere in the Next World he is still waiting to hear from them!

His inability to catch on to English humour, especially of my father's kind, is best demonstrated by what has become a standing family joke. My father told us all a fairly corny story about a traveller who arrived at a village and read the notice on a board which proclaimed:"Five miles to the next village and if you can't read, ask the blacksmith!" We all laughed dutifully, except Yevel. His face never lost its serious, contemplative look. Many hours later, however, when we had all forgotten the joke, Yevel started laughing uproariously. "I've got it," he spluttered, almost choking with mirth, "supposing the blacksmith couldn't read!" If ever anyone in our circle is slow in the uptake, that's what we say to them.

He used to wear quite expensive clothing, silk shirts and ties from Liberty's but I noticed pretty soon, with the schoolboy's perceptive eye, that these became worn and torn and that he tucked the cuffs out of sight to hide the ragged edges. His speech was most peculiar. Although he was quite fluent in English, his pronunciation was still very foreign. He used to say "desn't" instead of doesn't and, like most continental Europeans, his "w" was always pronounced like a "v". Despite his lack of our sense of humour, he laughed frequently when, as it seemed to us, there was nothing to laugh about.

There was an inner tension there that could only be released by these somewhat violent outbursts of laughter. Apart from the adverse experiences of his ghetto life in childhood, which had no doubt left their mark on him as on thousands of others, he also had a rather unhappy background of divorce, estrangement and consequent loss of contact with an only daughter. He had a yearning for things artistic which, foolishly, we sometimes mocked, loved classical music and, at one point, took up lessons in painting. This latter, we suspected, was to give greater credence to his pitch as an "artist", in the picture business, his main source of income. We still have a portrait of my mother, painted by his art tutor.

During the Twenties and Thirties, my mother kept in touch with her father in Russia. He was undergoing great hardships, possibly because of the authorities' attitude towards religion but probably much more as the result of the difficulties experienced by millions of others at that time in the Soviet Union. Whatever the cause, my mother felt it her duty to help him financially and regularly sent a ten-shilling or pound note by post.

They corresponded in Yiddish, which is a spoken language, picked up by the Jews during the middle years of their life in the diaspora. It is based predominantly on a medieval form of German, with a fair proportion of words of Hebrew origin, plus a smattering of many other languages. It is written in Hebrew characters, using some of the "silent" letters as vowels. It is written from right to left and it always intrigued me to watch my mother writing it in longhand so quickly and fluently.

We have a photo of my maternal grandfather, in which he is sitting among an assembly of village elders, bearded to a man but otherwise it is like a photograph of the whole school in the playground.

The Village Elders

We also have a studio portrait of a highly spiritual man, with Yevel's rather hollow cheeks and high cheekbones, gazing at the world in childlike wonder. He died some time before the war, thus cutting off all further connection between my mother and her homeland.

Apart from taking us for walks along the front, our parents also took us on charabanc outings, one of which impressed itself upon my mind for reasons which will become apparent. It was a journey billed as "Henfield Circular", you went out one way and came back another. The day was boiling hot, it was an open bus, the leatherette seats were burning hot and shining in the sun.

Sitting on this overheated form was like having your bottom baked in an oven. Maybe I had also had unsuitable food for dinner. Whatever the causes, I began to feel searing pangs in my bowels, the sure sign of oncoming diarrhoea. I have no wish to disturb the reader's tender feelings, so I will content myself with recording that my father had an unpleasant and delicate operation to perform when we finally reached the cafe where we were to have our tea. (I still have the instrument he used - a penknife - in my possession). Needless to say, Henfield Circular became and remains a standing(!) joke in our family.

My two elder sisters went out to work as soon as they left school. With no certificated skills, the main form of employment available to them was as a shop assistant. They all made friends easily and of course I knew most of their friends very well. My sisters had the knack of retaining their friends, some for their lifetime. They were mainly schoolfriends though I don't think any of them actually came over to my school when the boys and girls amalgamated, as they had left school by then. But they came to our house and that is where I got to know them.

Helen was dark-haired, slim and very fashion conscious. It was this latter tendency that often brought her into conflict with our mother. Fashion demanded silky clothing at all times; commonsense and health protection prescribed heavier, woollen garments in colder weather, especially undergarments. Hence the clash. I don't think the conflict was ever satisfactorily resolved.

Her lively mind was always at work, making critical remarks, cracking jokes sometimes at other people's expense, including her brother's. She was never lost for words, had a sharp eye, a quick wit and a talent for recording her ideas and writing stories and poems and, in my view, could have become a writer. But her talent was never fully developed because of lack of educational experience. Her attendance at school was sporadic due to bouts of real, or maternally imagined ill health. She exercised an influence on me far greater than she or I imagined.

Gertie was the only blonde in the family. Her round face and generally rounded exterior led many to believe that she was German. She was the only one of us who, I feel, was artistically gifted. I still have one of her coloured drawings in an issue of the class wall newspaper which she did during the short period when she was in the same class as myself. She became quite a good swimmer and we swam out to sea, together, on many occasions.

Etta, the youngest member of the family,. was auburn-haired and, like Gertie and me, on the plump side. She also became a competent swimmer. She was the only one of us who won a scholarship to the Varndean Secondary School. This was in 1929, just after it moved into its new building, now occupied by the Comprehensive School. She showed considerable academic ability and, through her, I got a closer insight into the mysteries of Secondary education.

It is difficult to assess what effect being the only boy in a family of four children had on my character and behaviour. I know when I complained, as I often did, about one or other of my sisters, to my parents, I was always told that, as a boy, I should give way to the girls. But I don't think I felt very gentlemanly towards them.

The Goldman Children. ca 1925

From about 1928 my father's earnings became very intermittent and uncertain and money worries were beginning to loom large. The source of my father's business troubles was not far to seek. The generally depressed state of the econonmy was no doubt the real culprit but, of course, I knew nothing of that. What I did know was that, as he was unable or unwilling to do the canvassing himself, he had to rely on someone else. And in those hard times, such a job became extremely difficult. Consequently he was always looking for a canvasser. When he managed to get one, he or she either turned out to be unable to get "copies", or else they were able to do so and could thus make demands on my father which he was unable to meet.

Among the former was "Uncle" Jack, a Lancastrian, who lived with Auntie Cassie in Bournemouth. He came and stayed with us and did some canvassing for my father. He even took me out with him once, when I had nothing better to do, to show me the ropes. He could talk the hind legs off the proverbial donkey, but he was not very successful in Brighton. People in the expensive flats that he canvassed were not very impressed with this fast-talking northerner; his nasal tone and artificial self-confidence barely concealed his anxiety. Because of his lack of success, he didn't stick it very long. He liked his drop of booze and soon retreated to the nearest pub.

On the other hand, there was one particular woman canvasser, a certain Miss Alexander, a large, fat lady of uncertain age, who was quite phenomenal. She had the cheek of the devil and would knock on doors that few others would dare to approach. However, her successful sales manner and aggressive methods were also employed in dealing with my father, who hadn't the iron in his soul that, in my view, marks the successful businessman.

She was considerably better off than we were, though she never seemed to spend any money and dressed atrociously. The strength of her position was that my father could not do without her. She was able to demand payment even for those photographs which did not yield orders and, throughout her working time with him, she consistently made a great deal more than he did.

Eventually, the only way my father could make ends meet was by borrowing from the bank, with the house as collateral. It served to cushion us from the worst results of his financial difficulties, but of course it could not go on for ever. That we had this valuable piece of property was due to the fortuitous circumstances at the end of the First World War, when business in Weston was easy to come by. But using it as security for loans could only have one end.

The bounds of Brighton were not the limits of my horizon, during my youth, for Brighton was a centre where we received vistors from other towns and also a base from which we visited those same friends and relatives. There were two main towns involved in this traffic: Birmingham and Bournemouth, though we once went back to visit the Rudys in Weston-super-Mare. Birmingham figured most prominently , as it was my father's home town. His parents, or

Bobba and *Zaida* (granny and grandpa) as I called them, still lived in their small semi-slum, in Essex St.

It was a two-storeyed terrace house, with outside lavatories in the common backyard. The large range, fired by coal or coke, provided both warmth and cooking facilities. It was a cosy, snug retreat where all seemed secure - but unreal. In the bedroom upstairs, there was a patchwork woollen overlay to the *perena*, a soft feather quilt, an old-fashioned country cousin to the modern duvet.

We met the rest of the Birmingham branch of the family at my grandparents but also in their own homes. There were the Shusters: Auntie Hettie, my father's sister, and her husband, Sholem (Sam), who made a very precarious living as a tailor. Of their large family, two older sons died early . But that still left two sons and three daughters.

Sholem was a short, cheerful, rather podgy man, who bulged at the waist. He had a whitish, stubbled face, a protruding lower lip and dark brown, soulful eyes. One felt that his cheerful exterior was a protection against life's .hardships. He made his own suits and always contrived to look smart. I remember him in light grey slacks and blue blazer and a shirt with fancy cuff-links. I also remember the warmth and affection with which he and his wife and children always greeted us.

He liked his glass of beer or stout, especially Guiness. He could seldom afford the latter, though. My father was once travelling with him on a train when a waiter from the dining car, carrying a frothing glass of golden liquid, popped his head round the compartment door and asked nobody in particular: " Was yours a Guiness, sir? " The agonised look on Sholem's face and the way he moistened his dry lips when he had to ignore the question, were, my father told me, pathetic to behold.

Then there was my father's younger brother, Harry and his wife, Pauline (Auntie Polly). Their daughters were Malka (Molly) and " Little " Cassie who, I believe, was named as a compliment to Auntie Cassie. I well remember her arrival, as we received a wire in Brighton, announcing the birth, when I was about 7 or 8. Harry had had no training for any specific profession or trade, as was indeed the case with the majority in those days. He worked with my father on several occasions but he also did a certain amount of honorary work for the local synagogue. By great good fortune, when the post of *Shamas* (beadle) came up, he got the job. It seems he was totally satisfactory to the community and so he remained in this position, which carried a house and other perks, to the end of his days.

My father's other siblings were Auntie Leah, who died young and Cassie's twin, Sadie, who lived with her husband and (eventually) four children in Leeds. I cannot remember them ever visiting us in Brighton and we never went to Leeds. It was not until we moved to London that we got to know them.

What we noticed about all the Brummies was, of course, their accent. This, together with the Glaswegian of our Scottish cousins and the Hampshire accent of Auntie Cassie's daughter, Mary, must have had an unconscious effect on our perceptions of the language. All were different from our "Brighton Cockney."

From the warm and excitable atmosphere of our Birmingham sojourns, in a dark, dirty, industrial city, it was a great contrast to go down to the serene, clean, well kept and airy atmosphere of Boscombe, the "Hove" end of Bournemouth. During the war, Auntie Cassie had got to know an elderly, rich but ailing man (a non-Jew) whom she eventually married. I don't think he survived to see his daughter, Mary, who grew up into a pretty little blue-eyed blonde.

Cassie was small and thin, always dressed smartly and liked to pretend that she was a bit of a flirt, afterwards privately making fun of the men she encountered. Actually, I believe, she was quite a prude. The one fling she had, being the first - and last. But, very strangely, she took up with a north country type who apparently worshipped her and who lived in the same house but, we are all convinced, never had any intimate relations with her. He was a sort of protector and general help. We all called him "Uncle" Jack - as did my cousin, Mary. Jack was the canvasser reffered to above.

Auntie Cassie and cousin Mary lived with "Uncle" Jack in Parkwood Avenue, not far from the famed Fisherman's Walk, with its tangey avenue of pines leading down to the sea. Their home was a double-fronted, detached house, with a neat garden at the back. It was expensively furnished, though the antiques were probably imitation. I remember that in the lounge there was a huge tiger-skin rug which we eventually inherited.

I was always given a lovely little back bedroom, overlooking the garden and I usually found some small present in one of the drawers in the dressing table. One I remember was a box of superb "birds' eggs". These were sweets, probably marzipan, in the very realistic shape of the eggs of a wide variety of birds. There was always a servant and the house was not only clean but also had a certain air of luxury about it.

Auntie Cassie liked to take us out to tea, usually at Plummer Roddis, who later had a branch in Brighton (now taken over by

Debenham's). When I grew old enough, she would take me to their *thé dansants* and try to push me into asking one of the young ladies who frequented the place, to dance. They were all older than me and I was scared stiff at the prospect and never acceded to her urgings. But I loved the atmosphere and felt very grown up. I also loved the tea and cream cakes and scones which were provided lavishly in those days.

The whole atmosphere in Bournemouth was different from Brighton. It seemed altogether more sedate, old-fashioned and countrified. The little green, banana-like plants (otherwise known as Hottentot figs) that clung to the cliffs, gave the front a much more rural air. Fisherman's Walk was always a delight, with its paths strewn with pine needles, giving off a pungent scent. Then there were the chines leading down to the beach, narrow gorges, to the west of the town and, beyond these, Poole Harbour, a natural deep water area where small craft of every kind tied up; all so very different from the seaside I lived in and knew. A change is as good as a rest, they say, but I was always glad to get back to Brighton, with its familiar sights and smells, and to all my friends.

Auntie Cassie and Mary (and sometimes "Uncle" Jack) also visited us in Brighton many times. She had a strong nasal twang and a sly line in coy, naughty conversation. It was really quite innocent but it was a kind of hallmark. She seemed particularly fond of me but I found her reminiscences of me as a baby rather embarrassing, especially as she liked to dwell on certain intimate details, not normally referred to in polite society.

There was one activity we always undertook whenever Auntie Cassie came. We children all went off with her to pick blackberries. We took the tram up to the Dyke Rd. terminus, just opposite Tongdean Lane. From there we walked towards the Dyke, along a narrow lane, lined with blackberry bushes. Unfortunately we were never properly equipped. Neither Cassie nor my mother had any real idea of the practical necessities required for blackberrying.

All we took with us were paper bags which, when filled, were placed in another, larger, paper carrier bag. The discerning reader can well imagine what happened when the juice from the berries came seeping through and finally saturated the paper. On one occasion, we were all sitting down in a cafe near the station, enjoying tea and cakes generously provided by Auntie Cassie, to slake the thirst engendered by the picking process. Just as we stood up to go, the bag burst at the bottom. The sad fact is that the next time she came and the excursion was repeated, *the same thing happened*! We never brought home a full load of berries from these excursions.

We never visited Glasgow. It was too far away for our limited resources. But the Glasgow branch of the family made regular visits to us. Auntie Esther's visits with Arnold or Harold, or both (Uncle Mendel seldom accompanied them) were times of great excitement for us. Arnold was the younger of the two, but a few years older than me. Even in his youth he was attractive to and attracted by the opposite sex in what seemed to me an obsessive way.

His thick, black, wavy hair, very thick eyebrows, a bit like Groucho Marx - or Pavarotti, large bright brown eyes and red sensuous mouth, obviously drew the attention of the girls - even when he was still in short trousers. He also shot up, very quickly, from about thirteen, outgrowing his elder brother, who remained quite short in stature. It was mainly from Arnold that an important part of my education derived. Suffice it to say that I pronounced most of the rude words I knew in a heavy Glaswegian accent until I gradually realised what they meant "in English"!

Both he and his brother were pretty tough. They had grown up in the Gorbals, Glasgow's East End, and we southerners were soft by comparison. They taught me how to box and how to do long jump and, more interestingly, boasted about their prowess in sport and with the girls, suitably exaggerated, but no doubt with a kernel of truth in their boastings.

They came with me when I played with my friends. It was " a known fact " that the Scots were good at football and this gave them an instant status in my circle. This even carried over into cricket, played in St. Anne's Well Gardens. Arnold was bigger and probably stronger than any of us and adopted a leadership role, which my friends seemed to accept. Once when "Felix", the park-keeper, came to order us off the strip of ground we had adopted as a pitch, Arnold stood up to him and it nearly came to fisticuffs. At any rate, we were left in possession of the field. Arnold boasted, later, that he had "sent him off with flying colours".

As the two boys grew up into young manhood, their exploits took on a more adult and romantic turn. They became expert dancers, as they were both musical and could play popular tunes on the piano, by ear and had a wonderful sense of rhythm. On one memorable occasion, Arnold took me to Sherry's Dance Hall, at the bottom of West St., thought of by the more respectable citizens of Brighton as a den of iniquity.

We did not actually go on the dance floor, Arnold's pocket wouldn't run to that, but sat on the balcony upstairs and had a pot of tea. It was my first experience of a real dance hall and I was suitably impressed, but despaired of ever reaching the standard of dancing so nonchalantly accomplished by those on the floor below.

Esther would sometimes take us out to buy us a present, usually a book. She was not too pleased when I chose an expensive annual instead of the little children's storybook she had suggested. She was always dressed up to the nines and the boys also had a fashion sense from an early age. She had a dress shop in the Gorbals and, though she may have been somewhat flamboyant, she knew what suited her and, within the limitations of her background, she had, if not exactly good taste, then at least a flair, which certainly drew attention to her even in a fashionable resort like Brighton, which seemed to suit her persona.

On one memorable occasion, it may have been around 1928, we all went on a trip back to Weston-super-Mare, to stay with the Rudys. It was our first return, after about seven or eight years in Brighton. We children had, of course, developed almost into adolescence, in the intervening years. And, what is more to the point, had not seen much of our friends in that time.

Wolfie and I renewed our friendship and found that it had not been diminished by the separation. He regaled me with stories about gang warfare between the little cliques of boys who roamed Grove Park. He had great admiration for the leader of his gang, who apparently devised horrible tortures for any member of the other gangs they might capture. It was all in the mind, of course, I do not believe there was one drop of blood spilt or even any real animosity between the groups involved. They just loved the excitement and stimulation of the imagination which this sort of talk provided.

I must have been learning Hebrew at the time, because I remember instructing Wolfie in the intricacies of the Hebrew alphabet. This is amusing now, because he later became proficient in the language, whilst my at best imperfect knowledge has rusted, to put it mildly.

The Rudys also came to stay with us in Brighton, several times. Wolfie and I went on many walks, swam together and exchanged adolescent confidences. It was during this visit that I played my first games of table tennis on the table in the front room. The Rudys had, by this time, moved to London, where his father was employed by a furrier in a City warehouse. I later repaid the visit and stayed with them in their flat above the warehouse, at the top of the City building, in Great St.Thomas Apostle Queen St., where Mr. R. was acting as caretaker.

We had now both developed into young men of the world and our conversation ranged far and wide, inevitably including girls. He told me stories of the activities of the young people at his school, an East End Central School. They seemed a lively bunch, much more sophisticated and mature than us provincials. Living in the East End, with its ghetto-like atmosphere, was a rapid maturing process. His description of some of his schoolmates and their attitudes and behaviour brought visions of a different world to me. Both visits served to strengthen our friendship. The whole family, too, renewed and deepened their relationship, which had the other long term effect of cementing a friendship which lasted - for our parents - until their deaths. Wulf (as he is now styled) is still alive, indeed is married, with children and grandchildren and recently celebrated his Golden Wedding! We are still good friends.

One visitor whose sudden, unannounced appearances were always greeted with great glee by us children, was the Harry Gold I have mentioned before He was very young when we had first met him in Weston and had trained as a marine engineer on the Clyde where he served an apprenticeship but was something of a natural genius with the internal-combustion engine. He later rode racing motor-cycles for Dunlop. He was also a daredevil and loved to scare us with his pranks. He once terrified us all by walking along the rather narrow top of a wall with a sheer drop on the other side.

What a wonderful engineer that man could have been were it not for the business tradition of our community which seemed to offer quicker rewards. He had shown his natural business acumen when he worked, for a time, as a canvasser for my father. He did not stay with him very long, however, trying a multitude of ventures until he settled into the motor-car trade - a lifelong passion and a lifelong career.

One day, he turned up in Brighton, having taken on a job as a demonstrator at an exhibition in the Dome and he brought me one of the products he was selling, a set of Kliptico. This was a sophisticated toy that might be compared with Meccano. On another occasion, he brought us a His Master's Voice gramophone, also from a Dome exhibition. There were no electrically controlled ones then, you had to wind them up. We were delighted with this addition to our entertainment aids. He also gave us some records and these helped us in our early attempts at dancing. It would be nice to recall that the gramophone had one of those gigantic horns, shown on the HMV logo, with the faithful dog listening in. But this more modern, portable instrument did not have one.

On one occasion, he arrived with his wife, Rose, in a bull-nosed Morris, open to the sky and with a canvas hood that could be put up in inclement weather. Great was the thrill of riding along the front in this vehicle. My two sisters and "Auntie" Rose sat in the back, where the boot would be in a modern car but where, in those models, there was a dickie, with seating for two - or three at a stretch. He drove us off to some beauty spot or place of interest and regaled us with tea - and talk. On the return journey, the girls fell asleep in the back whilst I tried not to doze off in the hot front seat, full of tea and cakes and jumbled but silent thoughts.

It may have been especially when Harry Gold came, or simply when there were quite a few at our house for some special occasions, but I certainly remember large parties crowding the front room. For the meal, the table would be extended to its fullest length and Janie's best efforts, and they were considerable, I can tell you, would weigh the table down and the noise and excitement would fill the room as completely as the guests did.

At my Barmitzvah party, for example, after the table had been cleared and folded away, Harry called upon Sholem, who was also present on that great occasion, to sing a song. "A little bird tells me", he shouted, above the din, "that Sholem knows some Yiddish songs." Sholem was persuaded to oblige and revealed that he had, indeed, got a fine baritone voice. He sang *Rozhinkas mit Mandeln* (Nuts and raisins) a very popular Jewish folk ballad, and I noticed tears in my mother's eyes as she remembered how it was in the old days when she was a little girl at home with her parents and the whole family used to sing it together.

There were also other contacts and acquaintances, outside the family circle, whose influences were significant. One of these, a rather Dickensian character who came into our lives for a few years, in the Twenties, was an old former friend of our parents, a certain Mr.Jacobson. He had lost his right leg but walked on his left leg with remarkable speed, with the aid of a wooden crutch. A thick cluster of pure white hair framed his otherwise completely bald head and his brightly twinkling little blue eyes fixed you from behind a pair of thick pebble glasses.

He made his living as a herbalist with a little shop somewhere in town, a forerunner of our modern health food shops. This fact alone made him of special interest to my sisters and me. But he also had a wonderful line in stories about his past adventures. If one believed him, he had been everywhere, seen jungles and forests - and met their inhabitants face to face, sometimes in combat! And we did believe him, every word. I remember my youngest sister sitting fascinated on his knee, drinking it all in. We somehow believed him capable of anything - good or evil.

His wife had left him some years earlier, because of ill-treatment, it was rumoured. By the time he caught up with us again she had returned to him, somewhat chastened. She had a little wart with a hair on the end of it on the left side of her chin and wore pince-nez spectacles. She was meek and submissive; he was domineering and most unpleasant to her, which his subtle tone only served to underline. Was he seeking revenge for her desertion or perversely taking his physical handicap out on her?

He was very excitable, argumentative and cynical and I had an instinctive desire to oppose his views, or perhaps his whole attitude to life. One of his favourite sayings, in his thick foreign accent, was:" I see your meenink", when on rare occasions I was able to get an idea across to him and his tiny eyes would twinkle again through the thick glass.

There were also a number of rather frightening characters roaming around Brighton, in those years. Perhaps our fear was due to our own provocation and devilment or, in some cases, a too vivid imagination, but they certainly invoked fear. One was an old man with a long beard. Whenever we saw him - provided we were at a safe distance - we shouted:"B.e.a.v.e.r !" and ran like mad. In his anger, he used to smash empty bottles with his steel-tipped walking stick.

More dangerous, however, were the men of perverted minds and habits. One of them displayed himself once to my sister, in St. Annes Well Gardens. A detective came to the house and my mother and sister went into another room to speak to him alone. Mother told us that she was wondering how he would broach the subject and she was impressed with his delicacy. He had asked my sister whether the man had shown "his private parts", the first time any of us had heard such an expression. It was always a matter of some curiosity to my schoolfriends and me how adults referred to matters which we boys spoke of in the usual crude terms handed down from generation to generation in school playgrounds up and down the land.

There was one man whom I sometimes accidentally met in my lone wanderings, usually in one of the parks. To this day, I cannot fully explain why I feared and loathed him. He had high cheekbones, hollow cheeks and his eyes seemed crafty, menacing - evil. He used to engage me in conversation, the content of which was irrelevant. It was his whole slimy manner and insinuating movements that nauseated and alarmed me. He never did anything overtly unpleasant but I always had a powerful feeling of unease in his presence, especially when there wasn't another soul in sight. I always avoided him when I could and, when I couldn't, ran away in sheer panic as soon as I got the chance.

Another unpleasant encounter occurred, once, in the amusement arcade on the lower promenade, where the subway to West St. is now situated. I was looking into a large glass case and was so engrossed that I hardly noticed a plumpish young man who had sidled up alongside. As I turned in his direction I found that he was gazing at me intently from behind a pair of thick glasses. With his small, fleshy, red-lipped mouth attempting an ingratiating smile, he grabbed and squeezed my hand and murmured just two words: "Dear boy!", before I was able to snatch my hand away in disgust and blurt out: "Getoudovit !"

With Mother(R) and Auntie Cassie

SCHOOLDAYS

We had arrived in Brighton some time before my fifth birthday, so it was not long before I had to attend Crown St. Infants' School where I began my formal educational career. The main entrance was in Crown St. but we beginners had to enter the school the back way, via a private house (owned by a chimney sweep) in Dean St. The following year I took my younger sister with me, when she reached school age; a boy of six trusted to take his five-year-old sister all the way from Powis Square to Dean St. unaccompanied by an adult.

There was one very large hall which housed four classes. How on earth the teachers managed to teach in what must have been a babble at the best of times, I have no idea. I was rather badly behaved and can remember one incident as evidence of this. A girl sitting in front of me was said to be wearing a wig and I was one day tempted to lean forward and tip the wig off her head. In another class, at Christmas, presents were displayed on a side table. As soon as I saw this, I stopped whatever I was doing and sat up straight in order to signal my undying devotion to all that was obedient and well-behaved.

Alas, the teacher's understanding of little boys was more than a match for my sudden conversion. "It's no good sitting up now", she said, " you should have thought of that when you were being naughty!" I have endeavoured to follow that precept in the decades which have followed, with perhaps limited success.

After Infant School, came the Elementary School. The girls went to St.Stephens School in Borough St. which was technically the Girls' Dept. of Christ Church School. The old building still stands, looking rather like the front of a small chapel. Etta's scholarship to Varndean, meant that she was the one member of the family to have a Secondary (Grammar, in today's terms) education. Despite this, the rest of us went on to show various talents which we developed in later life.

The all-boys school I went to was Christ Church. The building, in Bedford Place, still stands - it is, indeed, a listed building. It has now been converted into a theatre used by the New Venture Players. It bears the date of its foundation, 1841, above the front door. The actual inscription, just legible under the crumbling paintwork (recently refurbished) is: "Christ Church Schools - 1841". I started there on April Fools' Day 1924, a few months before my eighth birthday. I left, as was normal in an Elementary School, at the ripe old age of fourteen.

It was a very small school and, despite its name, had little connection with the church next door. I seem to remember that the classes were intended to have two age groups in them. Some of us progressed rather faster and at about ten found ourselves in the top class. I remained there for four years, having failed the scholarship examination.

The Elementary School was the child of the latest reform of the original state education deriving from the 1871 Education Act. Its purpose was to give free, compulsory schooling to workers' children, up to the age of fourteen, society having expanded to the extent that large numbers of literate people were now required to fulfil a whole number of more or less humdrum but essential functions in a modern, industrialised country. As will be seen, some of the teachers had a broader, more liberal approach.

There was also the Secondary School, catering for middle or lower middle class children with intellectual bent, and producing not only clerical and other more literate workers, but also laying the basis for an even smaller number who might go on to more academic or technically skilled spheres by attending university or other forms of post-school education. There was a small fee for these schools but there were also scholarships available for "bright working class children" covering, eventually, some 20% of the intake. These scholarships were based on an examination remarkably like the infamous eleven-plus of post-war notoriety.

Christ Church School was an old, part-stone, part-brick building, including a red-brick extension, built in the early years of the century. It had an impressive teachers' entrance and a narrow pathway down the north side leading to the smallest playground you have ever seen and to the side door, which was the pupils' entrance. The Head's study was just inside the main entrance.

During lessons, the hall was divided, from floor to ceiling, by a partition which was only pulled aside for special occasions, a whole-school assembly or a public performance of a school play - which I remember better than any other use. The right-hand side of the hall, on the other side of the sliding partition, was used as a classroom.

When I first arrived, the Headmaster was a Mr. Ridout, who was soon followed by a Mr. Hawkins who remained Head for many years after I had passed through the school. He had a pronounced country accent and often wore shiny leather gaiters in winter, from which characteristics I deduced that he came of farming stock.

The teachers were: Miss Newington, Mrs. Spicer, Mr. Gordon, and Mr. Smith, who taught the top form. These were later joined by

Mr. Russell for music.   Discipline was much stricter than it is today and both the strap and the cane were much in evidence when occasion demanded.   Lines were also given as a standard punishment.   There was, nonetheless, a good deal of bad behaviour, though it does seem that smaller schools suffer less from this.   Here I should also mention the School Board man, who visited children at home to check up on their absence - or truancy !

A bell was rung at the beginning and end of playtime as well as at the end of each session and the start of afternoon school.   When I was in Class III, I was promoted to bell-ringer, my first public appointment!   The school day was from 9 to 12 and from 2 to 4, with two hours for dinner.   At playtime we either played football in the postage-stamp playground or milled around the school or out onto the pavement.   There was a bakery shop in Cross St.,off Bedford Place, just below the school.   It was owned by a Mr. Richardson, father of one of my classmates.   When we had the money, we often bought "a pennorth of stale cakes" there - three for a penny!

Football in the playground was a classic example of schoolboy inventiveness.   The total size of the playing area was about 13 feet by 13 feet - the size of a largish drawing room.   A tennis-ball was used and even penalties taken.   Although we also had football one afternoon a week in a local recreation ground, the level of our team's performance just about matched the size of the mini-playground.

In my first year I had Miss Newington, a tallish, slim young lady, who could be both strict and motherly almost at the same time. On one occasion, she gave one badly-behaved little boy the strap. Unfortunately for him it seems that she overheard his remark that, "She didn't hurt."   She called him out again and repaired the omission. And yet, that same afternoon, she was mothering a boy with earache and when someone seemed derisory at this mollycoddling she asked him if he had ever had toothache. " Earache is twice as painful", she told him, "so think yourself lucky you haven't had it!"

It was fascinating for me, many decades later, when I was president of Brighton Teachers' Association and presiding at a tea for retired members, to find that a certain Mrs. X sitting at one of the tables was that very same Miss Newington.   We had a lively gossip about old times at Christ Church.

That year I recall learning the beginnings of arithmetic and spelling and of revealing my greatest weakness, handwriting.   It also emerged that I couldn't sing.   I'm told every class has at least one "growler"- and that was the beginning of my ostracism from music lessons.   There was apparently another boy with similar difficulties and we were both called out to sing a duet, "Golden Slumbers". The rest of the class enjoyed it hugely.

Next year we had to go downstairs, to the dreaded Mrs. Spicer's class. Known as "Ma Spider", she always insisted on being called ma'am. She had lost her husband in the war, from which I deduce that widows were allowed to retain their posts, small compensation for the loss of a loved one - and breadwinner. She wore a brown wig over her grey hair and always wore the same skirt. It was ankle-length and made of brown serge, held up by a severe belt. It was topped - always, it seemed to me - by a frilly white blouse. This may seem incongruous but it was the only frippery she allowed herself.

She was liberal with the cane and feared by all, even (as I learnt later) by the Head and the rest of the staff. She once set us to learn a poem of enormous length when she had to leave the class alone for a while. I enjoyed it and can still recall the feeling of pleasure I had in learning and reciting it.

Another memory of that year is the play we performed for the whole school. It was a dramatisation of that old favourite, "A Christmas Carol". I played the role of Mrs. Cratchett. When I brought in the turkey I was supposed to say: "Done to a turn!", and snap my fingers. But no matter how often Mrs. S. showed me - and she was very good at it, with her long smooth fingers - I just couldn't snap mine. This role was, however, the start of my school drama career, the most enjoyable and influential of all my school experiences

Behind that classroom there was a cookery instruction room, where girls from my sisters' school used to come every Wednesday to be taught by an Irish teacher, Mrs. Unsworth. They were kept strictly segregated from us boys (a kind of sexual Apartheid) and even had their own playground on the other side of the school. Later on, the meals they cooked were available for sale to boys who found it difficult to go home for dinner.

I was always provided with fruit by my mother, usually a banana. This was often supplemented by the aforementioned stale cakes or broken biscuits or sweets. My favourite sweets were toffee, gobstoppers and licorice. But at midday I always went home to a good, hot, cooked meal. Whatever else we were short of, we were never short of food.

My greatest joy, on the way to school, both in the morning and the afternoon, was kicking a tennis ball all the way down the hill. My route was from Powis Square diagonally across to St. Michael's Church, then right along Victoria Rd. and left down Montpelier Villas, kicking the ball all the way. I kicked it against the concrete ridge which held up the railings of the houses. The ball went forward, struck the ridge at an angle and I dashed forward to meet it, repeating this manoeuvre practically to the school gate. From Montpelier Place I continued on to Temple St., ran down Temple St. and only picked the ball up when I got to the busy Western Rd.

I was nine-plus when I escaped from Ma Spider and went up into the third class. It was here that I first met someone who was to have a very great influence on my development, both as to character and outlook, as well as on my theatrical and literary leanings. He was W.A.Gordon, a Scotsman from the Highlands and member of a proud clan.

His nickname, of which he was well aware, was Wag. He was soft spoken (except when angry and he could put on anger, when it suited him, like you put on an overcoat). He was on the short side but very wiry, quick and active and full of fire, dark and ruggedly handsome in a very Celtic way. He was just eleven years older than me, although I did not know it at the time.

His lessons were dominated by drama and poetry and my incipient attraction to poetry was set on fire by his enthusiasm. I have been addicted to both ever since. Many years later, he told me that the methods he was pioneering then were still regarded as avant garde well into the Sixties.

I can still see him, striding from the door (he always strode, never walked), his plus-fours flapping, and reciting: "John Gilpin was a citizen of credit and renown", placing metric emphasis on the syllables in time to his pacing. This was to explain iambic pentameters to us. How that esoteric term still rings in my ears.

The only specialist teaching in the school was music, or rather, singing, from which I was soon excluded. For practical subjects, we went, every Wednesday, to a woodwork centre in east Brighton - later the home of the Secondary Technical School, in Hanover Terrace. One teacher was an elderly man, with greying hair, a long thin red face and a Lancashire accent, who pronounced sugar "shugger" and seemed to detest little boys. We disliked each other intensely. I was not gifted in this direction and these lessons were a penance, though I made a matchbox stand which we used at home for years.

One afternoon, on my way to this centre, I was just crossing Dyke Rd. at its junction with Clifton Terrace, just opposite the church, when I was struck by a car. I was in one of my dreamy moods, perhaps not even realising that I was crossing a road. Little damage was done, as the driver pulled up in time. But my leg was cut and he took me to hospital to have it attended to. My mother had a fit when the hospital sent for her.   But - I got out of woodwork that day!

Wag was a pretty good disciplinarian.   He was able to control us by his considerable personality but, like all the others, he used the strap when he thought it necessary.   We boys accepted it then though, today, I am totally opposed to corporal punishment.   One naughty boy sticks in the memory because of his name, Riccamboni.   "Rag-and-boney" was his natural nickname and he was a constant nuisance to everyone.

On one occasion Wag had probably slapped him.   He dashed out of his seat and made for the door.   "Where are you off to?"   "I'm going home to tell my mother."   "Oh, yes, you'll go home, alright, - on a stretcher!"   This brought such a laugh that the boy was shamed into resuming his seat.   Wag often referred to this incident in later years, when we became good friends and colleagues.   "I wouldn't recommend that method, today", he said, "but it worked!"

There was another boy who was sometimes in trouble, but harmless really, who became a schoolboy boxing champion.   He turned up one day in his best blue suit, looking very smart.   It turned out that he was to go to London to receive his trophy.   I believe Wag remarked that that was the right way to use his energy.

Some of the other boys I remember were Jack Hageman, a good looking sprightly lad who played Prince Hal to my Falstaff in Henry IV Part I, when we were both in Form III.   I was a pretty obvious choice for the fat buffoon.   How well I remember the scorn in Jack's voice as he called me: "You fat man, you barrel of lard", lines which, I am sure, he relished.   From that day forth my old nickname, "Fatty", gave way to "Fatman", used by my friends with affection rather than detraction.

Our first teacher in Class IV was a Mr A. E. Smith, a tall, fair, slim man who was in his thirties and his grey eyes gleamed behind his rimless glasses.   He was also very fast at football but one boy told me that he could easily get the ball off Mr. Smith's feet because, at that speed, he was not fully in control of it.

Although he did not have Wag's charisma, he also used modern methods and had a certain impish humour, though this could disappear rapidly when faced with disruptive behaviour.   He also did not hesitate to use the cane when he thought it necessary, for instance if he heard a boy calling him "Smudger".   Unlike Mr. Gordon, he had a degree in English.   Although Mr. Smith spoke with a Sussex accent, he once told me that he didn't like "Brighton Cockney".

When performing the three witches scene from Macbeth, once, in front of the class, I declaimed: "When shall we three meet again?"

in what I thought was a witch's voice. "You sound" said Smith," like Mr. Brown asking his wife what's for supper!" "In thunder, lightning or in rain", whined the other witch. "That", he quipped again,"sounds like Mrs. Brown, telling him".

At this time I was increasingly fascinated by the use of language, both in its spoken and written form, of which essays were the fashionable exercise. But verse and anecdotes were also encouraged. I can remember two pieces I did for Mr. Smith. One was based on our study, at that time, of Hiawatha. I was intrigued by Longfellow's use of repetition to get his effects, couplets like:

Listen to his words of wisdom,
Listen to the truth they tell you
　　　　　or
Sailed into the fiery sunset,
Sailed into the purple vapours.

He also set us an essay on: "Parents and children." As luck would have it, I was reading Jerome K. Jerome's: "They and I", at the time. The book deals with J. and his wife and two children, so it could not have been more apt for the subject of my essay. Having thought about the morality of lifting whole chunks from the book (and the possibility of detection) I marched out to the teacher and put the question to him.

He saw nothing wrong in my using the *ideas* in the book, where they suited my purpose, but sieved through my own perceptions. This was a lesson that I have never forgotten. The question is not whether one should copy other people's ideas but, rather, whether it is possible to create something original out of ideas absorbed from others and experiences involving interaction with others.

Mr. Smith and Mr. Gordon also tried to extend our cultural horizons. One dinner break they brought along a record of someone singing an aria from *Lohengrin* (Wagner of all things with which to beguile the ears of Brighton's rude youth!). I still remember that we were first told the final words of the song: *My father Parsifal the Knight and Lohengrin my name.* Those who had volunteered to attend this session listened dutifully and tried to look interested. This attempt to please became much more genuine when *Lohengrin* was followed by a more popular classic and we were encouraged to tap our feet to the accentuated rhythm. These days I find it difficult not to do that when the rhythm excites me.

Mr. Smith was absent one day and it was whispered around that he was at a teachers' conference where he was "chairman of the union". Sure enough, when I, myself, achieved the exalted position of President of the Brighton Teachers' Association, there was his name, recorded in the archives, as president, way back in the Twenties.

Mr. Smith left us during my first or second year in the top class. It was at this point that Wag, who took over from him, became a major influence in our lives. After all those decades, I feel that influence still. Perhaps his most distinctive characteristic was his iconoclasm. He inculcated into us a healthy suspicion of all established wisdom and thus encouraged the enquiring mind, the requisite of a truly educated person.

It was his natural libertarian attitude, coupled with the undoubted influence of Shaw, that produced this anti-Establishment attitude of his. I always felt he wanted to puncture our acceptance of traditional norms. On the other hand, I don't think that he was the kind to commit himself to any movement or to active struggle against the things he criticised.

He introduced us to Shaw and Wells, those two gurus of the discontented, in the between-wars years. Shaw, a fellow Celt, no doubt had a special attraction for him. He was a consummate actor and he once read the whole of Shaw's St.Joan to us, over a series of lessons, reading every part himself. I shall never forget his magnificent anger when, as Squire Robert de Baudricourt, he rages at his steward. I can still see him, eyes flashing, mouth working, almost spitting blood: "Thirty thousand thunders! Fifty thousand devils! Do you mean to say that that girl........ is still here?" But he could coo like a dove, when the part demanded it.

He also introduced us to J. K. Jerome's "Three Men in a Boat", a book I must have read and re-read dozens of times since, and it still sends me into fits of laughter at the irresistibly humorous descriptions of human frailty and pretensions. Here was satire, easily available even to the young, and we lapped it up. In fact, I was deputed to choose an extract each Friday afternoon and read it to the class as a sort of end-of-week treat. And using my voice for public purposes has been a task that has been assigned to me with remarkable frequency since.

I also learnt a number of poems, many of which I can, even now, repeat. And the odd thing is that for day-to-day purposes my memory is very poor. I take this as proof that, when the motivation is strong enough, such defects can be overcome. I love the beauty of the poetic form and the images which the sounds evoke. We learnt poems like *Ships of old Renown, Wander Thirst, Sea Fever, Cargoes, The Bells of Heaven, I Love all Beauteous Things, Abou ben Adam, Lord Ullin's Daughter, Drake's Drum, Requiem, The Moon is up, The Highwayman.* I can also recall Wag reciting to us: "Q'elle est belle ma Marguerite!", with flaring nostrils and uplifted face. As it happens, there was a girl called Margaret in the class and she may well have thought that he was reciting it just for her. What a performer! Some of the above may not be great poetry but they fired the imagination of a sensitive schoolboy.

One method that Wag introduced of bringing out and developing our confidence in public speaking and our ability to run our own affairs, was the class meeting. We learned all about chairmanship, the formalities of debate and minute taking. I was soon installed as class minuting secretary and learnt the secrets of Reported Speech and the Past Perfect. As I was also a frequent participant in the debates, I was kept pretty busy. There is no doubt in my mind that this experience started me on the road to a confident espousal of my point of view.

There were some amusing incidents during these meetings and some interesting revelations. There was the occasion during the 1929 election, when we had a directly political debate. During someone's speech, I noticed a significant look passing between Wag and the Head (who happened to have strayed into the classroom - perhaps intentionally). Were we making a point which had already been raised in the staffroom, I wonder?

Another time, a young woman student on teaching practice had been listening in to a debate on: "Should students be allowed to practise teaching in schools?" She intervened to make the point that such practice was a form of experiment and that much had been gained by experiments. "That sounds fine", said I, in replying, "but why should we be used as guinea pigs?" Such freedom to express our views was certainly not the norm in schools in the Twenties.

Our insistence on clarity of speech is highlighted by another incident. One boy had been regaling us with his views, punctuated by the frequent interposition of :".. as a marrer fact..". When he was finished, the chairman called for questions. One boy asked him, with all appearance of seriousness, the meaning of "marrow fat"! We always started our remarks with the formal: "Mr. Chairman and gentlemen". Each proposal had a proposer and seconder and, if possible, an opposer and seconder. But it was not all debates. Sometimes boys would describe their holidays or games would be devised and controlled by the chairman. How well I remember The Truth Game, in which everyone was on their honour to answer questions truthfully.

This was one of the rare situations in which Wag might occasionally intervene with what he called his power of veto which, incidentally, is how I first learned the expression. This might be when questions, sometimes quite innocently, went too near the knuckle. Wag had once been seen with a young lady, walking along the front and a boy asked him how close to each other they got. This was not the kind of question Wag vetoed. He revelled in it. The answer in inches was: "Nought upon one squared".

There was a negative side to Elementary Schools which, though mitigated if you happened to have an inspired teacher like Wag, nonetheless was inimical to an all-round education. Firstly, the range of subjects was limited: no serious science of any kind; no foreign languages; no public examinations that could be a stepping-stone to further or higher education; even those subjects that were taught depended very much on the skill and interest of the teachers concerned.

At one point the Head decided to give us a few science lessons. I remember only two of them. In one, he filled a tumbler of water to the brim, placed a piece of thin paper over the top, firmly pressing down on the rim. Then he turned the tumbler upside down. The paper held! A miracle? No, surface tension. In another lesson, he demonstrated what he called the inertia of motion. First, he bent his forearm right back, so that the back of his hand was above his shoulder. Then he placed a small pile of pennies above his upturned elbow. What next? Well, the trick was to whip his forearm forward at speed and catch the pile of pennies in his hand. It worked.

Now, although Wag was a near genius at English-related subjects and interested in sport, at which he also excelled, other subjects were of less interest to him and one, Geography, he obviously disliked. Indeed his favourite ploy, when we were being obstreperous, was to darken his brow and, in a voice of thunder say: "Get out your Geography books!"

One result of this has been a lifelong block, where science and maths are concerned. Maybe, like many another, I had no special leanings in that direction in the first place and no encouragement at home. I have striven to overcome this handicap but with only limited success. Who knows what I might not have achieved with the necessary encouragement in these subjects.

Art was not one of my talents nor anything connected with neatness, tidiness or an ordered, systematic approach. I have always been more on the inspirational side, relying on imaginative instincts and deep, emotional urgings. So it is not surprising that the appearance of my work, including my written work, left much to be desired.

With still life, Wag's method was to get us to draw an outline of the composition and then pencil in the detail before adding in the colours. My outlines were always misshapen and the filling-in increasingly cramped and difficult. I was unable to judge shapes, sizes and positions. So I greatly admired the skill of people like my friend, Bob, who could paint a delicate flower with all the different shades of colour and make it look like the real thing. This was a closed book to me.

It wasn't too bad in class, where my work could be decently hidden. But one sunny day, in the summer of 1928, as a treat, Wag took us out to the beach, with drawing paper pinned to boards, to draw a ship that had caused some interest in the town. It was anchored some distance from the shore and to me it looked like a small black smudge on the sea's surface. But other pupils apparently saw enough of it to put in the various spars, masts, hull and other details. Wag, ever generous, bought us all an ice-cream but when he looked at my effort he said: "For God's sake hide the thing, turn it over or something, so that no-one can see it"! I was only too willing to oblige.

I wasn't too bad at design, though. We were taught how to cut stencils and stipple them in with a hard-bristled stencil brush. I once cut an individual stencil for my folder, in the form of a monogram. I used my initials as human figures, attaching little heads, arms and legs to them. I shall never forget the pleasure I had when a visiting inspector, looking closely at the design, remarked: " I see. Good idea. The thin Leonard (letter L) and the fat Goldman (letter G)." Praise. And in art!

Wag used to introduce subjects to us arising from some current interest or fad of his. (I told you his teaching was inspirational). He seemed to have taken a fancy to lettering and he showed us how Roman capitals were written, which I have never forgotten. I still use this technique, today, when I want to hand-print capital letters for something special.

In those days fountain pens, though available, were not allowed and, of course, biros had not been invented. So it was the old traditional pen and ink. To put my predicament in a nutshell, when my mother once came to see Mr. Gordon he told her: "If he was in one corner of the room and the ink in another, he would somehow get it mixed up in it!" Yes, my fingers were grubby but my imagination was all aglow.

Drill was a weekly affair and no doubt helped to keep us active. It may have given us a sense of acting together which, perhaps, stood me in good stead when I was conscripted into the army during the war. As there was no gym in the school, we were marched up Montpelier St. to Victoria Place where there was a little drill hall.

Despite my bulk, I think I did rather well at drill and the associated games. I can clearly remember jumping the highest in the class, 4'6" to be exact and, as luck would have it, doing it right in front of the local inspector who happened to be visiting the class at the time. He was a Mr Watters, a compatriot of Wag's, and as I cleared the bar, I fell right at his feet.

Wag took us for the weekly games afternoon. A footballer of some ability, he had little interest in cricket, so it is the former that looms largest in my memory. We marched up to the "rec" in Dyke Rd. (just beyond the present 6th Form College) got out six-foot poles which we stuck in the ground as goalposts and the game could begin. Wag gave us no serious training in football techniques. We simply kicked the ball around and enjoyed ourselves.

We were only a small school and our team was regularly beaten by large margins by the other, much larger, schools. As the biggest boy in my year, I used to lead the march up to the ground and was also the captain of the team, in my last year. This meant that I had charge of the ball over the weekend and had to carry it to the match. The school colours were brown and blue and I won't record what the boys from the other schools called them!

Some boys wore shin-pads though I do not recall ever wearing them. The football boots in those days were pretty shoddy. The toe-caps were of very hard, shiny leather. The join, where they fitted the upper, was often harsh and uncomfortable. The studs were of small, round layers of cork or leather and frequently came off. The nails with which they were affixed to the soles often poked through inside, causing considerable discomfort. But the actual joy of playing outweighed any such petty irritations

.Wag played for two local sides, at the weekend: Yale (in bright canary jerseys) and Vernon Athletic (in stripes). He always played at right-half (if any readers still remember those outmoded positions). We used to watch him whenever we knew he was playing, though he never told us beforehand. I was not all that impressed with his skill. He was fast and played with a kind of wild abandon that perfectly revealed his artistic nature. I wonder how much time he spent, if any, learning and practising the arts of ball control.

We also had swimming lessons; a boy would lie, face downwards, over a chair and try to simulate the movements of the breast stroke. My bulk made this exercise extremely uncomfortable and eventually I taught myself to swim, in the sea. I never have really mastered the breast stroke, only the "over-arm thrash".

Considering its size, the school was quite outstanding at swimming. At the local schools' swimming gala, held at the North Rd. Baths, we gained both the champion swimmer's medal and cup as well as the team cup. My friend, Hammond, though a year younger than I, won the champion's race and he and I and two others came first in the 4 x 33 yards team race while I came second in the 100 yards race in my age group. The winner of that race was a boy from Middle Street, another very small Elementary School.

When Hammond and I emerged from the baths, after the gala was over, we were seized by a group of our classmates and an attempt was made to "chair" us out into the road. As this involved hoisting us onto somebody's shoulders, they had considerable difficulty with me and the whole episode finished in a welter of laughter and general bonhomie. Then we all trouped down to the fish-and-chip shop to celebrate.

I still have the photograph that Wag had taken of all our entrants, with the medals, cups and shield that we had won between us. Hammond went on to become schoolboy champion of Sussex at 100 yards. He and I were invited to become members of Hove Shiverers Swimming Club. Unfortunately my parents vetoed this because it finished too late in the evening and meant a long journey home in the dark.

Some week or so later, Wag took us all out to celebrate, with a raspberry-and-cream tea at the Lyons tea shop which was situated on the corner of Old Steine and St. James Street, where the Job Centre now stands. We were all in high spirits and Wag told us stories of his youth.

As so many of us were keen on swimming, Wag arranged for us to use the baths at St.Luke's School one night a week, for training and general enjoyment. There was a little coterie of us swimmers; a somewhat different circle from the footballers, though a few of us were in both. After a while, the girls came along too and it turned into quite a social event. The baths were much smaller than the North Rd. ones (now The Prince Regent). But their very smallness made the whole evening more intimate, with more of a family atmosphere.

I also remember the evening when Wag turned up with a couple of friends, not intending to swim. When he saw us all splashing around and obviously enjoying ourselves, however, he was tempted to go in, himself. But he didn't have a swimming costume with him. I was the only boy whose swim-suit was big enough, so he offered me half-a-crown (2/6) to borrow it. I lent it to him, of course, but I wouldn't dream of taking the money. He looked quite comical in it, almost indecent, as it was far too large around the waist.

There were seasons for out-of-school games, like conkers and marbles. The conkers season obviously depended on nature's bounty. I don't know what determined the onset of marbles. Both seem to have been more popular then than they are today. I was never very successful at conkers. Other boys had methods of toughening up their horse-chestnuts by baking etc. to make them practically invulnerable. Mine always seemed to split at the first or second whack. Nonetheless, the ritual of collecting your conkers, by throwing missiles up into the trees, then piercing them with a skewer, threading string through the hole and securing it with a knot, never failed to entice.

With marbles, it was the fascination of the shining metallic colours, as they winked at one from the shop window, that made the small ceramic spheres so attractive to the schoolboy's eye. I couldn't afford to buy many and, sadly, I didn't win many other people's marbles all that often. But it was exciting fun to watch boys rolling them towards a boy who had set up his marble by sitting open-legged with it in front of him and then to join in, all other cares forgotten.

French cricket was another unofficial sport we often played when there was no space or time to play the real thing. One boy had a cricket bat with which to defend his feet, at which others shied a tennis ball. No runs were scored but the successful thrower was rewarded by taking over the bat and the process began all over again..

Another innovation in our class was the wall newspaper, *The Tatler*. We were encouraged to write up any incident, however trivial it might seem at the time, as a news item. We could also submit essays done in class, if we thought they might be of general interest. Drawings and sketches, in colour or black and white, cartoons, funny poems, limericks, experiences out of school, were all welcomed. One of my closer friends, Bob, who later became a successful journalist, was the editor.

Decades later, when I met up with Wag after a separation of some thirty years, he was a tutor in a teachers' training college in Bognor and I had already started teaching in Brighton and, to my delight, I discovered that he still had the whole Christmas 1928 edition of *The Tatler*, pasted onto large sheets of brown paper.

Eagerly scanning the sheets, I came across my essay, "On picking up a piece of Downland turf." It is fascinating to be able to read a childhood piece you wrote over sixty years ago. The subject matter was a description of an outing many of us had had, on the Downs, with Wag. As it happens, he had lent me a small haversack to carry my sandwiches in and - I am sorry to recall - I left it behind and only discovered the loss when we were all well on our way home, though still on the Downs.

I went back and the others waited. The main motivation was to recover Wag's property, but in the essay I made a great fuss about the remaining sandwiches that were left in it, thus maintaining my buffoon's role as the class fat boy with an exaggerated interest in food. I never did find the haversack, but the incident and the people I met on the way and the bull's hooves I *thought* I heard, all made excellent "copy". I remember one comic poem in which a boy called Mott made fun of Wag: "...... his ears do wag etc" to which Wag replied with rhymes about: "... silly dot, what a clot etc." Puerile schoolboy stuff, you may say, but it says much for the atmosphere in that class and how far the pupils knew they could go.

The class was divided into "tribes", each of which was named after a Red Indian tribe. There were the Mohicans, the Hurons, the Crees and the Sioux. We did not get points for our work and achievements but "scalps". On a large board behind his desk Wag fixed a "totem pole" which he had asked one of the woodwork teachers to make. It was highly varnished with an impressive, brightly-coloured animal's head at the top.

On either side was a space for recording the scalps gained by each tribe, in each of the disciplines included in the competition: sport, the various subjects, debating etc. Each term, the scalps were totalled and the winning tribe had its colour painted onto the totem pole in a broad strip. The whole thing looked most impressive and we all took it quite seriously. We could lose scalps, too, and at the end of the week there was a little ceremony of adjusting the scores. There was also a highly varnished, wooden tomahawk, used as a chairman's gavel at class meetings.

At special drama evenings, to which parents were invited and for which quite attractive cyclostyled programmes were produced, each class in the school put on a performance. This was the most enjoyable aspect of my schooldays. I couldn't get enough of it. Since those days, my love of acting and the theatre has never dimmed. I remember with great clarity every production in which I took part. I have already described my earliest roles, Mrs. Cratchett, in *A Christmas Carol*, and Falstaff in *The Fight at Gads' Hill* from Shakespeare's *Henry IV Part I*.

In the latter, I am pleased to relate, I was not considered fat enough for the part and had to have a large cushion stuffed under my costume. Nonetheless, I was the obvious candidate for the big buffoon. Indeed, it was as the boy who played that part, that Mr. Smith seems to have remembered me. When I contacted him some years ago, it was the first thing he referred to in his reply.

The next play was about a gang of rogues under the leadership of a toff whom they called "Toffie". Wag took the part. They had been very successful because Toffie always foresaw the next move. They had stolen the eye of an eastern idol, which eventually comes, itself, to get them. "I did not foresee it," says the Toff, as the curtain falls.

When the school became a Senior Mixed, we had the obvious advantage that girls could now take female parts. The first mixed production was "Five Birds in a Cage", about four passengers who get stuck in a lift, with the liftman making the fifth character. This was the only play I can remember in which I did not take part, and so was able to enjoy it thoroughly from a seat in the audience. The next play was one that I recall with particular clarity. It was called: "The Man in the Bowler Hat".

I played the chief Villain, with Leslie Phipps as my Bad Man assistant, browbeating an innocent and very matter-of-fact Mr. and Mrs. Brown in their own drawing room, in order to discover the whereabouts of the rajah's ruby. Their very ordinariness drives him to apoplexy and he collapses defeated, when he discovers that they've left it in a left luggage department - and have lost the ticket. Playing the leading role in a farce like this gave me a tremendous thrill; the dim blur of faces in the audience, sitting expectantly still; the bright lights on the stage; the feeling of command that a confident knowledge of the lines gave you; it was all a deply rewarding experience, which in some respects has coloured my life since.

We played this piece several nights to considerable acclaim and even took it elsewhere, on one occasion to the Blind School, where I believe Wag was the voluntary warden. After this performance, the chairs were cleared away and we all danced to the music of a gramophone. The pupils were all boys and Wag had taught them to dance - with him and with each other. On that night the only girls there were those in the play and a few others from Christ Church who had come along to help or to watch. It was a very jolly and enjoyable evening and we had no embarassment in dancing with the boys, most of whom were partially-sighted.

One incident stands out. A boy approached Wag to ask him to dance with him, innocently imagining that he would agree, as he always had on similar occasions in the past. But Wag was dancing with one of the girls, Hetty Drew, I think it was, and brusquely cold-shouldered him. I don't think he meant to be unkind but the incident confirmed what we thought we already knew about Wag - and girls.

But special performances such as these were not the only drama that Wag used in his teaching. We also had a kind of free drama. He would give us a theme, or ask us to assume a character from a play we were reading, suggest a situation and we had to take it from there, adlibbing as we went along. Creative drama, which left deep impressions and enhanced our ability to think on our feet

Another out-of-school activity was chess. Wag taught a few of us the game and I soon became quite competent at it, in schoolboy terms, and enjoyed it immensely.   Together with a few friends, I joined the adult Christ Church Chess Club, situated a couple of doors down from the school and whose secretary was a Mr. Brookes who was acquainted with Wag and was possibly a former pupil of the school.   On one memorable occasion, he picked me to play for them against some mid-Sussex club at board 30.   I lost, of course.

At one point, Mr. Gordon introduced two pairs of boxing gloves into the class and we were encouraged to use them as playtime entertainment. It was my first introduction to the sport and I must confess I liked it. There was little viciousness among the boys (though there was some bullying) and this type of fighting was presumed to enable us to work out our aggression in a controlled way. I think it worked to a large extent. Wag occasionally put the gloves on, himself, but usually only with the most competent

In keeping with his open approach to the pupils, Wag often took us out walking on the Downs and this was the beginning of a love of the outdoors, and of Sussex in particular, that has stayed with me and, I know, with many of the others, for the rest of our lives. Poynings was a favourite area but we ranged far and wide. We got to know the Devil's Dyke too, and a number of other beauty spots. As I cast my mind back to these rambles, I can still smell the grass in spring, see the lambs in the fields, the bright yellow flowers on the gorse bushes and feel the springy downland turf under my feet. This wind-in-the-hair feeling was all a part of our experience and contributed to a particular outlook, by which I am still influenced, even in old age.

In 1928, the local authority decided to create Senior Mixed Schools. Christ Church was already, in theory, one school, comprising Crown Street Infants, St. Stephens Girls Department (as they called it) and Christ Church Boys' Department, which I attended. So the procedure was fairly simple. The girls from St. Stephens came over to us.

Now this was quite a revolutionary event. The whole atmosphere changed, Wag was in his element. He had really only reckoned with teaching boys when he started. But it did not take him long to size up the new situation. He was already rather hero-worshipped by many of the boys. Now it was the turn of the girls to fall for his charm.

There was a whole new range of names that entered into our thoughts and conversation. There was Molly, a pretty Jewish girl, who made up rather heavily, as was the fashion at the time, Margaret Laplain, who became rather popular with some of the boys. She told me later that an uncle of hers from the North was something big in the T.U.C. My sister, Gertie, was also in the same class as me for a year. She was very good at art and one of her paintings is in the copy of *The Tatler* which I referred to before. My essay on the adventure on the Downs (published in *The Tatler*) was, on Wag's request, copied down by her, so it is in her handwriting, not mine.

The participation of girls in the class meetings brought a new element into this activity. We had a girl chairman (there were no "persons" in those days) addressed as madam chairman and speeches were introduced with: "Ladies and Gentlemen". Games, like the truth game, for instance, became that bit more daring and amusing. I remember one boy, who had been seen carrying a girl's satchel, was asked why he had done this. Quick as a flash came back the answer: "Because I'm a gentleman". We all thought this a very clever reply, a good example of thinking on his feet.

Soon after the arrival of the girls, we started country dancing sessions, after school. This became a very popular activity. I always stayed but usually watched rather than taking part. The only dance I remember was "Gathering Peascods", which I believe is still a popular number today in what is now called folk dancing and I can still remember the tune. Wag took part in all this with enthusiasm.

Later, ballroom dancing succeeded country dancing in our out-of-school activities. This kind of dancing appealed to me more than the other and I took my first steps in what has proved an enjoyable social activity ever since. My sisters had been teaching me such steps as the foxtrot and the quickstep at home and so I was able to start with some confidence.   From being an after-school activity, dancing developed into a real social occasion, reserved for the weekend. With a boy called Legg on the drums and cymbals and Ernie at the piano we had the perfect embryo dance combo.

Some of us boys, without actually thinking it through consciously, used to go round and pick out the less attractive girls, who seldom got partners, and ask them to dance. Many of them were uncertain of the steps as they may have come from a milieu where dancing was not a common practice, so we were very pleased with ourselves when we managed to "get them round" successfully. Such was our burgeoning confidence - or conceit!

We watched Wag's progress on the dance floor with avid interest. Which girls did he favour? Which did he dance with most often ? Which did he hold just that little bit more tightly?   He must have been aware of our interest in the matter but it did not seem to worry him in the slightest. There was a great deal of speculation about him and his social and emotional life. But we never really found out very much. If he was seen with a girl, the intelligence was passed along the grapevine at speed. But you couldn't embarass *him*.

There were also various innocent liaisons between girls and boys in the class. And these, too, were watched by the rest of us. It was really quite a little adult society, in miniature: not a bad training in social and emotional relationships for later in life.   Many of us were either too girl-shy or too cautious to attempt such liaisons. Not that we didn't want to.   Some of the maturer and more sexually advanced boys were very willing for the rest of us to know that one of the girls in the class was "their girl".   But the first hurdle of chatting up even the most friendly of the girls was an impossible one for me and some of my friends to surmount, at thirteen.

The girls, themselves, had a problem too.   For most of them, especially the less attractive, it would have been painful to make up to a boy and be repulsed, though some of the more forward ones certainly tried. Some boys semed naturally popular with the opposite sex, either because of good looks or personality.   And we accepted this as the natural order of things.

When the girls first came into the class, I suppose Wag decided he ought to lay down the law and tell us all "how it was going to be". After a long and serious explanation of the purpose and method of his teaching and the kind of order he expected, he finished by detailing the punishments that offenders would accrue, with corporal punishment for the boys, as the final sanction. One girl was bold enough to enquire: "And what about the girls?" "The girls", he said, in his best histrionic style, "I will lash with my tongue." He could not resist the temptation thus to dramatise his intentions.

60

Another disciplinary method introduced at about the same time as the girls' entry to the school was the appointment of prefects from among the pupils. I don't know whether this was a snobbish attempt to copy the Public or Grammar School image or whether it was an exercise in a sort of spoof democracy. Needless to say, the prefects were hand-picked, not elected. A small group of senior pupils were promoted above the rest of us. To my mild surprise, I was not among the chosen.

I don't think they were very effective. Indeed, I cannot remember any serious misbehaviour that the staff could not have handled on their own. But one incident, in which I was directly involved, stands out in my mind. The bell had gone at the end of playtime and the twenty-odd pupils in our class were settling down somewhat noisily before the teacher arrived.

As team leader I felt some responsibility for good order and was remonstrating with a boy in my team (tribe). At the height of our altercation a couple of prefects came in and, as they saw it, caught me in the act and promptly booked me to appear before their council. With Wag also in attendance, they awarded me a hundred lines for causing a disturbance.

My attempts to explain what really happened were brushed aside. This was doubly galling because Wag lent his authority to this injustice and the prefect concerned was my friend, Ernie Bale. The whole affair might have ended there and then if I had sensibly complied with and carried out the punishment. Some devil within me, however, determined that I would hit back by writing lines that consisted of insults to the prefects: "Stupid prefects, silly prefects etc..." repeated for the whole hundred lines. Retribution followed.

The Head called me into his study and, for only the second time in my school life, I got the strap. When I returned to the classroom, Ernie and the others were looking very smug. But later there was some evidence that he was rather ashamed of his part in the affair and, oddly enough, it did not, for very long, interfere with our friendship.

School bullying is nothing new. I well remember being set on by a group of kids from another school, though I must admit it was more taunting than physical. There were also boys in my own school who could be unpleasant when we were on our own. It was usually older boys who, though no larger than I, were more developed and considered I was fair game. It was probably "only playing", as they always claimed. I wonder though, whether there was not some anti-semitism involved.

FRIENDSHIPS

Friends and acquaintances play a far greater role in a young person's life than they may realise at the time.   I can see now the emotional impact that my involvement with certain others of my age had upon my attitude and behaviour and I can trace back aspects of my present feelings to their influence.   You want to belong, to be accepted, perhaps even to entertain and amuse and to respond to similar efforts from them.   Of course there's nothing premeditated or clearly thought out; it's all very subtle and understated.   But no account of my early life would be complete without reference to my numerous friendships and other contacts.

Roy Watts was one of my closest friends.   He was a tall, good-looking boy with crisp, dark, curly hair and a permanent suntan. He was known affectionately to all as Negro, soon shortened to Neek. He even signed his articles in the Tatler as, Negro.   He was the most popular boy in the school. Later in life, Roy was one of those brave Englishmen who rallied to the cause of Spanish democracy and volunteered for the International Brigade. He died on the battlefield. His death was a tragedy that deeply affected my early adult life.

Bob Black was another friend. He was a very gifted artist and writer. Of medium build, thin and wiry, he had lank dark hair, riveting eyes that blinked incessantly and long, pointed fingers, that seemed magically inspired when they held pen, pencil or paintbrush. Bob was editor of *The Tatler* and it was his insistent work that helped to make it the success that it was.

We often went rambling on our own and my most enduring memory is going out in a threesome, Bob, Roy and I, on many a Sunday.   Once, we sat upon a hilltop overlooking the Weald and all of us feasting on the sandwiches which my mother had given me. She was always over generous in these matters.   Sunmaid seedless raisins were one of her (and my) favourite fillings.   As we ate we looked down on the tiny villages below and picked out one where we would have our tea.   They knew a waitress in one of the teashops, they said, with that look that teenage boys adopt when talking about girls.

It worked very well.   They had eaten from my lunch, now they were going to treat me to a slap-up tea.   Drinking in the country air and working up a mighty appetite, we marched down the hillside and into the tiny cafe. Bob grandiloquently rang the tiny handbell on the counter and, sure enough, out tripped a pretty, rosy-cheeked waitress, whom Bob addressed by her Christian name.   The tea of buttered scones, bread and butter and jam and pastries - and pots of tea, too, of course - was wolfed down in no time. Bob was already working by this time and so had the money to pay. On other occasions, there were incidents involving trespassing and even being chased by irate farmers, in good old traditional style; though I must say that at such moments we hardly appreciated tradition.

There were many other friends and acquaintances that I remember with some sentimental regard. There was Ernie (the pianist) who, with his classic good looks, was much favoured by the girls. His father was the proprietor of The Princess Victoria, on the corner of Regent Hill and Upper North Street. He told me, with some pride, that it was a Free House, that is, it was not tied to any one brewery, which meant that his father was more independent than most pub landlords. He also came to us once or twice. I remember my mother asked him to play *In a Persian Garden*, which seemed to be the acme of her musical preference. As we did not have the music, he was unable to oblige but he entertained us with pieces which he did know and after that was always a welcome guest.

He played the piano in a group when he left school and later became a professional actor. This did not surprise me because his natural abilities came out very clearly in the play where I was the Chief Villain interrogating the Browns. As Mr Brown, he got more laughs than I did, without even trying. Indeed, I remember that one of my chums in the audience was quite indignant about this, nudging his neighbours and whispering something like, "Never mind him, watch Goldman. He's the funny man." I know this because my sister was sitting next to him.

Another of my friends was Billy Mountain, a fair-haired, attractive looking boy, small of stature but remarkably good at athletics. Billy's prowess as a runner came to the fore one summer's day as we were practising for the sports at Dyke Road Recreation Ground. I was in the two-hundred yards' sprint which I confidently expected to win. Contrary to appearances, I was quite a good sprinter. However, on this occasion, Billy quickly took the lead and all I saw of him for the whole of the race was his back and, try as I might, he stayed ahead and beat me by many yards. Bill is the only one of my former schoolmates with whom I am still in contact. Until recently, he always returned to Brighton for his holidays, as he loves the place.

Another boy worthy of mention was Lewis. He was crippled, perhaps from polio. He had one withered leg which was encased in an iron frame and he had been provided with a special bike, with one revolving pedal, balanced on the other side by a fixed one. He manipulated this machine with considerable skill. But what was perhaps more remarkable, was that he joined in all the rough-and-tumble of life in a boisterous boys' school without fear or particular consideration by the other boys. In short, they accepted him and made little or no distinction because of his disability.

There were two other boys of my acquaintance, who won scholarships to Varndean - or York Place as it was for most of the Twenties. One was Philip Ball, whose father was manager of the news agents and post office in Preston Street. He gave his son plenty of intellectual stimulus and Philip was the outstanding brain of the form. Whenever I visited them, we always played interesting games and I could feel the whole underlying, cultural atmosphere of their home.

Another of my close friends at the time was a boy whose name is an excellent example of how nicknames were formed at school in those days. He was Gordon Thick. Now, today, such a name has obvious connotations. But not then. So he was first, Stick, then Sticky, then Sticky Legs and, finally, Gammy Legs or just Gammy. Gammy and I struck up an acquaintanceship because there were times when we were both lonely, usually in the evenings when our other friends were occupied elsewhere.

He was very small, tiny in fact, and we must certainly have looked a very odd couple indeed. But we were intellectually suited. We discussed everything under the sun and, when we got bored with discussions, we devised a rather cheeky game. He would start crying and I, pretending to be his elder brother, would explain to any sympathetic passer-by (and there was usually someone) that he was feeling unwell, that we had a long way to get home and that, of course, we had no money.

This kind of begging had a certain limited success and I suppose we spent the loot on sweets. We had a code name for this game, which I have forgotten. At any rate, we soon tired of it and probably began to feel some pangs of conscience at the deceit. Gordon had won a scholarship to Varndean but we still continued to meet. I once went to his house to ask if he could come out to play and his mother, perhaps thinking, "Fancy this big chap showing such disappointment that my little Gordon can't come out", could not suppress a smile.

These pupils at Secondary School brought us a breath of a different, more disciplined, more structured education. I certainly felt that it was at an impossibly high standard, beyond my abilities or inclinations, which says much for the false educational ideas that were around at the time, as my subsequent development has proved.

Another acquaintance was older and just about leaving Brighton College when he and I became acquainted. His real name was Clarence but he was known as Codey to family and friends. He lived with his parents and elder brother in a house in Montpelier St. I believe his father and brother were accountants or in some similar profession. I know they let the basement flat to the family of another one of our crowd called Aubrey.

Codey was a large, raw-boned young man, with a grin to match and a sense of fun that sometimes overstepped the mark. I believe he was thought of in his circles as something of a wild boy but I found him very friendly and easy to talk to. He and I were part of the group of youngsters who used to disport themselves on the beach, usually with a football or playing leapfrog, which I describe in greater detail below. We were all experienced swimmers and went in the water from early spring to late autumn. Codey and I used to swim out, on a calm, warm day and, when some distance from the shore, tread water and hold animated discussions about our future hopes and plans. I'd like to meet Codey again.

I could go on describing my other many and varied acquaintances but the above will have to suffice as representative of all their personal influences I experienced. If this book seeks out a few of those surviving (!) I shall be delighted.

In my 'Jantzen' with Mother (L) and Auntie Cassie.

THE SEAFRONT

Brighton's pebbly beach was second home to us during the summer months. Indeed, we swam in the sea from May (or even April) to September. I used to delight in running over the pebbles in my bare feet, just to show off, though it hurt sometimes. That was one way in which I could score off my Scottish cousins who had to limp painfully down to the sea. In most other ways they were tougher than I.

During the summer, the beach was covered with people in bathing costumes (not yet "swimsuits") sunbathing and, indeed, often getting painfully sunburnt. My parents could not swim, but my mother availed herself of every opportunity to don a bathing costume and sit in a deckchair in the sun. My father never did. He never even bared his legs. The nearest thing he did was to remove his shirt and sit in his sleeveless vest. He often placed a knotted handkerchief over his bald scalp to protect it from the sun. He had been bald as long as I could remember him.

When we first came to Brighton, none of us could swim. But we children loved the water. There are pictures of us in our striped bathing costumes, which buttoned up on one shoulder, but which were usually left unbuttoned. One photo shows three of us nonchalantly lying on our sides on the sand at the sea's edge, at low tide. But this gives little indication of how things were going to develop.

After we had learnt to swim and began to update our swimwear, we were able to enjoy the sea in all its moods. In those days you were not allowed to undress on the beach and nobody, not even men, were permitted to go topless. All swimming costumes had little skirts which provided a straight line at the bottom by covering, however slightly, the top of the thighs.

Then Jantzen brought out a men's costume that had large cut out pieces under the arms and round the back, so that there was an eight-inch strip of costume at the back though the front remained the same and the regulations were seen to be observed. Such costumes gave one greater freedom of movement and, of course, greater exposure to the sun, though even then we were sensitive to the discomforts, if not the dangers of sunburn. These new styles were expensive and had to be saved for over a long period.

In those days, I used to just run into the sea and start swimming without a thought in my mind about getting back to shore. There was never any oil on the beach or in the sea, then. On a calm day when the sea was smooth as a millpond, it was a delight to stretch the arms and kick the legs and go gliding forward in the supportive arms of the sea. In rough seas, with waves mountains high, what joy to dive through them and come out behind, as they rolled majestically inshore. What a spluttering and a shouting to each other in sheer wild abandon.

Because of the regulations, you either had to undress in one of the bathing huts provided or bring your own canvas tent. The beach we always used was the one between the two groynes to the west of the West Pier. It was known as Jim Hatton's beach because he had the contract for the bathing huts on that beach. He also provided life guards for the protection of the swimmers, bronzed young athletes who strutted around to the admiring gaze of the women and envy of the men.

Our own tent, whose heavy-duty canvas sides made it much heavier than everybody else's, was a square, dark blue structure, its walls held stiff by crossed wooden struts and held down by filling the internal pockets at the bottom of each wall with stones. Tents became little social centres and, together with families in neighbouring tents, we formed quite a coterie.

Friends used to come and use our tent as did visitors and relatives when they came to Brighton.   My sisters' and my schoolfriends came, too, if they did not have tents of their own. Games were played, meals eaten, gallons of tea drunk, either from flasks or bought from the many vendors whose kiosks proliferated at the back of the beach and who also sold ice-creams, sandwiches, cakes and chocolates.

These various stalls had to make their money during the season and very hard work it was, too. I shall never forget the man who once, whilst serving me with a tray with pots of tea on it, spilt some of the hot water on his hand. Taking a huge breath, he exclaimed: "Blimey it's 'ot!"   There were also a host of other small businesses and individuals who were all trying to make a living either on the beach or just behind it. I remember, in particular, the cockles-and-whelks stalls. "Try'em they're nice!" was one vendor's slogan.

People came trampling through the pebbles with heavy trays secured with straps that passed round the back of the neck, selling chocolate, sweets, cakes, biscuits, sunglasses, shady hats and so on. It must have been exhausting, especially in sunny weather, not to speak of the heatwaves I seem to remember as frequent occurrences.

There was also Archie, the handless artist, who operated some little distance from the steps that come down from the west side of the West Pier. He was small and slightly built with a thin-line moustache and was quite a remarkable man. Born with stumps instead of hands, he covered them with little mittens, grasped a special pen between them and did portraits and silhouettes. And very good they were, too. He used to get one of us youngsters to pose for a drawing in order to attract custom. He charged customers half-a-crown, about £4 by today's reckoning. I met him again a few years ago still looking quite young.

Apart from swimming and sunbathing, there were all sorts of other activities we engaged in. As I got older, I became more and more a part of a group of young men some years my senior. They were mostly in their late teens or early twenties and some of them lived not far from me and had tents on the same beach. They seemed to be shop assistants (my future destiny) or clerical workers of some kind.

One sport we developed was connected with a football which we threw at one young man who had stood upon a wooden structure, as we positioned ourselves all round him. It was not a very stable structure and the young man in the middle had to balance on it and ward off the ball at the same time, usually by punching it. As soon as he was toppled someone else took his place. Or else we would use the ball for heading practice. We would do this on a large circle on the beach, itself, probably making a nuisance of ourselves to other beach users. I remember meeting one of the players, a handsome young man called Aubrey, the day after one of these games, and comparing the state of our stiff necks!

Another game, in which my sisters and other girls joined in, was leapfrog. We played this on the hard ground above the beach where the boating pool is now but which was then gravelly open ground. It is remarkable how one improved at this with practice. In the end, I was leaping over three or even four people. As I had no sports shoes, I put on my ordinary leather ones. Without socks, these are pretty hard on the feet and the slightly uncomfortable feel of them is one of the most lasting impression I have of the game.

It was illegal to take quantities of pebbles from the beach, for one's own, personal use. On one occasion I was involved in this surreptitious activity. My mother had decided that she wanted some shingle to put in our back yard. An odd-job man agreed to carry out the perilous task of procuring the pebbles for her. I accompanied him just for the excitement. We went down there at dusk one evening and sat down side by side under the pier.

I can distinctly recall the smell of beer that he exuded and the rather dank and musty feeling that always seems to pervade the air under the pier. He had a sack with him and began slowly and cautiously to fill it with small handfuls at a time. With my inexpert assistance the task was accomplished and I heaved a sigh of relief as we got clear of the front with our booty.

The area above the beach was just a rubbly wasteland, when we first started going down there. Some time in the middle Twenties, the powers that be decided to develop this area. It stretched from the Fisherman's Hard to the east, right up to the Hove border in the west. As the work progressed many and wild were the speculations as to what was being built.

In the end, there was a children's paddling pool, the other side of the pier. On our side there was a boating pool, with rowing boats, paddle boats and motor boats. Further on were the sunken gardens and the bandstand where military bands played on Sundays. There was great excitement at all these changes and the different atmosphere they created.

Apart from the hazards of sunburn, there was the altogether more serious danger. I always thought of this as something that might happen to holidaymakers or "trippers" (what scorn there was in that word) but it never occurred to me that I, myself, might be in danger. On one sunny, breezy day, I was on a different beach from my usual one when I suddenly saw a commotion further down, nearer the sea. I ran over and saw a man getting first aid from a life guard, who eventually revived him. Those who knew about these things explained to me that there were strong undercurrents, not evident on the surface, which could drag you down before you knew it. This did not put me off, however, and I continued to enjoy my swimming without a care in the world.

Another unpleasant possibility was getting your foot cut on sharp objects, especially broken glass, which had been inconsiderately left lying around. I once got a very small piece in the sole of my foot but fortunately it was easily removed. Other friends of mine were not so lucky and one of them lost quite lot of blood from a cut foot and needed considerable attention.

One season we had a plague of jelly-fish in the sea. Many people were badly stung when they brushed against them and the primitive creatures had an unfortunate habit of coming up inside your swimming costume. One interesting phenomenon we observed was how different they looked in their natural habitat, the sea, from their appearance when washed up on the beach. In the sea they were like rather beautiful transparent parachutes. Out of the water they could have been thick jelly pancakes.

The promenade from the end of the Hove lawns to the Palace Pier was being broadened in my day. It is the best seaside walking parade of any seaside I have ever visited. Inevitably I judge all others by making the comparison. The railings have not altered from that day to this. I can stroke the weathered wooden poles and tell my daughter that I stroked exactly the same piece of wood all those years ago.

I have walked the promenade in all the seasons and in all weathers. On Easter Sunday, when the sun was shining on the thronging crowds, I got a tremendous feeling that it was all there for my entertainment. The young men in their enormously wide Oxford bags, some with bow ties and often wearing blue blazers, were shod in brogues, often two-coloured - black and white or tan and white. No adult wore shorts, at least not until the early Thirties. Plus-fours were also worn along the promenade as well as on the golf course.

The young women, usually in groups, wore short, knee-length dresses and skirts, with flowered designs on silky materials. And those high heels! The only man-made fibre that I knew of in those days was artificial silk, sometimes called art-silk, or rayon. So, for fashionable girls, silk stockings were the order of the day.

The clamour of the whole multitude, the mixture of local inhabitants and visitors of all types, stepping it out, looking for amusement, flirting, whistling or humming the latest tunes, swinging their arms or walking arm-in-arm, smoking - especially cigars or pipes - talking loudly and without inhibition, the smiling faces, people in various stages of inebriation, dogs tugging at their leashes and dog-owners tugging at dogs, it all brought vividly to mind the old cliché : *All human life is there.*

By contrast, on wintry days, with a stiff Brighton breeze whipping my bare knees (few schoolboys wore long trousers) with icy splashes of rain, the turbulent sea smashing down on the pebbles or crashing up against the low wall and over the railings to add to the wetness, I felt I was one of a very small number braving the elements and glorying in it.

What with the waves running high, forming a foreground for the piers, the loneliness of the walk, the impressiveness of the sea, with its grey-white crests and slimy green troughs, the noise of the wind and the cries of huge seagulls soaring overhead, it all formed a perfect background to the tumult of thoughts and feelings that raced through my mind. It was on these forays along the front, right up to Black Rock and beyond, that I formulated my ideas in a jumble of emotion.

At first, the path below the cliffs from Black Rock eastwards was a narrow kind of track covered in pebbles and often also with slippery seaweed that caused many a bruised shin when we tried to clamber along the rocks protruding from the sea bed at low tide. Some time in the late Twenties they started to build the undercliff walk. This made an enormous improvement and from then on my walks were less lonely, except perhaps in the icy cold of winter, for I went out in all weathers.

I used to enjoy walking on top of the cliffs, on the broad grass sward, which starts a mile beyond the Palace Pier and stretches right on to Black Rock. It was often cold and very windy but I loved it. On one such walk, I was going at a good pace when I heard footsteps behind me. I unconsciously quickened my stride and seemed to hear the footsteps quicken, too, which I must have felt was a sort of challenge and I really began to put on a spurt .

When I finally arrived at the little railings, sweating and breathing heavily, the young man whose footsteps I had heard was still some yards behind me. When he came up, we had a little chat. Apparently he was a seasoned walker and he told me that he was amazed at the speed I managed to get up. Perhaps I should have taken up athletics more seriously at the time, but somehow I never seemed to get much encouragement, knew of no clubs and, anyhow, would not have had the wherewithal to pay a subscription.

By this time I had outgrown the company of my sisters who had their own pursuits. But sometimes the whole family would promenade along the front. It was on these occasions that Dad might treat us to a ride on Volk's Electric Railway. It was never quite so thrilling as depicted on the advertising posters, thrusting its way through the waters! Its main value, as far as I was concerned, was that it saved us walking if we were feeling tired.

We also went out with relatives and family friends when they came down to visit us. And then we acted as guides. We might be treated to ice-creams or nougat, or nuts and raisins in little cardboard cartons. One relative used to take me onto the pier.

ENTERTAINMENT

There was a wide variety of entertainment in Brighton at that time. Along the front, apart from the various amusement arcades, the most obvious were the two piers. The West Pier was our nearest and the one I most frequently visited. It is quite a remarkable structure, the oldest of its kind in Britain, it is claimed. It not only served as a breakwater and as a place for ships to tie up but also - and more importantly - as a pleasure centre for visitors and inhabitants alike.

You entered through a turnstile from the promenade, paid your entrance money, 3d. or 6d. I believe, and started to wend your way seawards, past people sunning themselves on the deckchairs on either side of the windowed partition which ran for some fifty yards along the middle of the pier. You then approached the buildings, which formed the first bulge in the long straight profile of the pier.

This was the dance-hall and, behind it, the theatre. Having skirted this obstacle, you passed by a number of stalls of various kinds: shooting gallery, wheel-em-in (wheeling pennies down a sloping groove to try and land on a numbered square indicating how much you had won) and many more.

Beyond this again there were shops selling sweets, photographic equipment, ices and so on. Behind these was the open-air stage where pierrots used to perform during the season. One of the companies I particularly remember was Ouida MacDermott and her troupe. The comedian referred to her as: Oh, you Ida MacDermott! She was a singer of some ability and her rendering of the sentimental, *I'm a dreamer*, has lingered in my mind: the dream lover, *strong and tall*, who alarms her with his seductive charms; *he's ideal, but then he isn't real*. Quite! A sentimental ballad which mirrored the mood of the time.

They also did a sketch about a man plagued by his wife and daughter who where always asking him silly questions, like: "Are you having your tea, then?" when they could see him sitting there drinking it. In the end, in desperation, when his wife asks him: "Is that a new wastepaper basket?" he replies, in a burst of anger, "No, it's my new bowler hat!" And, suiting actions to words, he grabs it, turns it upside down on his head, scattering the contents all over him and stalks off the stage. During the show, a collection was made by one of the players shaking the collection box under the noses of those watching outside the auditorium.

Not far from the back of this stage was the great diving pool at the pierhead. This was used exclusively by a strapping amazon of a woman who, twice daily during the season, paraded around the pool area with a megaphone, shouting: "Any more for the diving at the bay at the head of the pier?" She wore a bathing gown over her tightly-fitting but decent swimming costume and really looked the part. We all followed her and soon a crowd had gathered at the scene of operations.

She mounted an enormous diving structure of Olympic height, removed her gown, took up the megaphone again and began her spiel. This consisted of descriptions of the dive she was about to perform and was always spliced with wit. The great height gave her more time for the mid-air athletics: jacknives, somersaults, the lot. She also told the audience that drowned women came up with their faces turned upwards whilst men came up with their faces downwards because, as she explained, they were ashamed to show their faces! There was a collection during her performance, too.

Right round the back of the pool, the cast-iron, openwork platform was used by passengers disembarking from the steamers and also by anglers. I never fished, myself, but many of my pals did. I disliked the smell, the wetness of everything, the insecurity one experienced by being able to see the sea beneath, through the latticework of the iron grill on which we were standing and the tangled jumble of the fishing tackle, rod and line, net and basket, bait and, worst of all, the slimy wet fish - if they had caught any - wriggling in the basket. But I pretended to like it for the sake of their company.

By far the most important items on the pier were the machines. There were the early pin-table machines and a whole gamut of other machines, most of which required the expenditure of a penny a go. They were encased in glass and had to be controlled from the outside by a handle or lever of some sort. In some you had to place a penny in the slot and it dropped onto a small platform from which you struck it and tried to land it in another slot. If successful you would get a packet of cigarettes or some other prize. You usually lost your money.

There were also some primitive fruit machines, apparently the only form of gambling allowed. But the piece de resistance, as far as I was concerned, was the one machine that is fixed in my mind for ever as a fascinating monument to human endeavour. These machines were also to be found in amusement arcades, and even in cafes, all along the lower promenade. There were some, for example, in a large arcade at the bottom of the steps opposite West St., were the present subway begins, which also housed all manner of other machines.

It was called The Little Stockbroker. It wasn't a real gambling machine *if you were in the know*. A number of us boys knew how the machines worked and won money on them consistently. They were of the fruit machine type but of a different design. There was only a small window, in front, through which three slanting coloured strips could be seen. Each had a name on it, denoting shares in a particular commodity and each commodity rewarded the player with a different sum of money, except for those labelled LOANS, TRUSTS and BONDS for which you got nothing. Blue was COAL, which paid out twopence, orange was RUBBER, worth threepence. There was a fourpenny one coloured brown, for SHIPPING. Then came pink, for TEXTILES - fivepence and, finally, gold for STERLING, for which you garnered the princely sum of sixpence.

The technique was simple. Penny in the slot, press the handle down, the disc spins round clockwise and comes to rest showing three new strips, an arrow pointing to the middle one. A small diagram at the bottom of the machine, where it was hardly noticed by the average punter, showed the whole of the disc in miniature and thus gave the exact sequence of the strips on the real disc in the machine.

Those of us who knew about this and profited from it were known as sharks. We knew that each time the disc spun it came to rest on the fifth strip to the left . We knew that each sequence of three strips was unique. So, by memorising the whole disc and the exact sequence of the strips, we knew exactly what was coming next.

We watched the punters putting in their money and, if they walked away when some profitable sequence was coming up, we stepped in, played until we had gathered in all that was available and then walked off with the loot. I was moderately efficient at this but there were some boys who were positive geniuses. I managed to finance my modest needs fairly well but some of them really made a lot of money. They could tell at a glance what was coming up, even when new machines appeared. They seemed to have the facility for learning the sequence in a trice. I greatly admired - and envied - them.

The Little Stockbroker

All was not plain sailing, however. The proprietors of the arcades perceived quite clearly that our activities were likely to discourage the genuine customers and their managers persecuted us with a ruthless determination. It was constant war between us. We had nicknames for all of them, whether on the Palace or West Piers or in any of the numerous other locations where these machines were to be found. And yet, despite their attentions, we managed to earn quite an income. Proper little potential capitalists we were! It was from this that I bought my first Jantzen swimming costume.

It seemed to me that there were dozens of other sharks competing with me and that the whole of Brighton must know of our activities. But when, on one occasion, during a class meeting, I was encouraged to describe the Little Stockbroker phenomenon, I was quite surprised to find how astonished and interested the rest of the class were, including Wag, who seemed intensely amused by the whole thing. He asked me how much I could earn and when I told him, probably exaggerating a bit, there was a gasp, perhaps of envy - or disbelief - from the rest of the class.

The West Pier also boasted a large theatre where I used to attend pantomimes at Christmas. I can remember sitting in the Gods, leaning over the rail, observing the faint gleam of the lighting on my own knuckles and drinking in the performance at the same time. It was there that I first experienced the age-old custom of interrupting the story with popular songs of the day, in those days usually of a more sentimental or comical kind.

But the theatre also had more serious drama, sometimes putting on special shows for schools. When *Macbeth* was being played, we first had a talk from Mr. Smith about the tremendous emotional impact of the murders. "If you cannot describe your feelings afterwards," he said, "I shall say to you what Shakespeare put into the mouth of one of his characters in *Julius Caesar*, 'You blocks, you stones, you worse than senseless things!' " Before the lights went out and the curtain went up, an actor who was to take the part of Macbeth came out in front of the footlights, already dressed for the part, and gave us a rather lengthy and boring talk about the play. This made the suspension of disbelief, necessary when one is watching a play, rather difficult, since we had seen and heard the principal actor out of character. And although we all appreciated being out of school for the morning, there was a certain disappointment with the whole performance.

On return, Mr. Smith asked us for our feelings about the dramatic events we had witnessed. We were dumb. As he had warned he would, he intoned the lines quoted above. However, as he put it, Macbeth had come out and spoken to us like a schoolmaster and then expected us to believe that he was a medieval Scottish nobleman, so there was some excuse for our lack of response

The Palace Pier was further away from my usual beat but I did go there from time to time. It was bigger than the other pier and had far more on it in the way of shops, stalls, games and other amusements. One I remember was a motor-driving game. You sat on a small stool looking through the window of the machine and facing a large picture which was moving downwards all the time. It contained an image of a country road with several twists and turns and a motor car whose direction you controlled by using the steering wheel in front of the stool. You had to steer the car and avoid the kerb edge. When you fouled this there was a loud blip. It was far more dificult than it seemed as the road was narrow, the steering awkward and you had no control of the speed. Even Harry Gold, an expert driver if ever there was one, got plenty of bleeps when he tried it.

The piers were also stations for steamers which plied along the

77

coast and tied up at their landing stages. You could see them from the shore, gliding back and forth, not all that far out. Apart from the fairly frequent trips along the coast to Eastbourne, Hastings, Bognor etc., they also offered a daily trip to Dieppe or even Calais and Boulogne (which Brightonians insist on calling B'loyn). If you were on the pier when a steamer tied up, you could see the passengers streaming on or off. I only once went on a trip.

Further entertainment was provided by Jack Sheppard's pierrots, a group who performed on a covered open-air stage with a proscenium arch, on the lower promenade to the east of the Palace Pier, roughly where the Big Wheel is now. Once when my Glasgow cousins, Harold and Arnold, were down with my aunt on one of their numerous visits and, with me, were avidly watching the show, a call came from the platform for volunteers to enter a competition for performance of an act. So these two extroverts marched boldly up and did a little sketch based on a pair of well known comedians. Much to our surprise, they were proclaimed the winners and carried their prizes home in triumph.

Apart from the pier theatres, there were two other main theatres in Brighton: the Hippodrome in Middle St. and our still beloved, Theatre Royal. The only turn I can ever remember seeing in the Hippodrome was Gracie Fields. What a performance! Her powerful, sweet, melodic voice could reach the highest notes, notes that sent shivers down your back, and this lent a special extra attraction to the popular songs she sang, many of them, it seemed, written especially for her. Her rendering of Sally could bring tears to the eyes of the most hardened theatre-goer. She could also make you cry with laughter. Her appealing Lancashire accent added just that touch of the exotic for us southerners.

As a burgeoning theatre lover, I visited the Theatre Royal as often as I could afford. One outstanding play I saw there was Shaw"s *St. Joan*, with the greatly loved Sybil Thorndyke in the leading role. At forty, she was playing a young girl of seventeen. I raved about her performance to my friends and anyone else who would listen. I also discussed the play and what I regarded as its message, with a member of the audience sitting next to me, a young woman with a rather snooty accent - and attitude, who considered Shaw "outmoded" (this was 1931!). I remarked that it was becoming fashionable to decry Shaw and she responded with, "Oh, I'm no follower of fashion." But I felt that I had scored a point and although I was only fifteen it gave me quite a grown-up feeling.

I suppose many people would consider films and cinemas to have been in their infancy in the Twenties. I can only say that they seemed pretty sophisticated to us at the time. All this exposure to handsome men and beautiful women, with dark shadows round their eyes, portraying exaggerated emotions and, when Talkies arrived, singing moving, sentimental songs, in situations of danger, romance, tragedy or pathos; what was its effect on the feelings and outlook of a sensitive and imaginative teenager, just beginning to emerge from his childish chrysalis and inch his way out into the world beyond his family and home?

I think I swallowed it all, gulping it down without sugar. I almost cried at the pathos of *Sonny Boy*, accepted, uncritically, the stereotypes in *The Cohens and the Kellys* and generally allowed myself to be enthralled and entranced, as I was expected to be. In the darkness of the cinema, sitting on my plush tip-up seat, I was in a kind of trance where only what was on the flickering screen seemed real. All the more willingly did I accept this fantasy world when real life was often painfully disappointing. The cinema was an escape, a soporific, a new religion. "The opium of the people"?

The atmosphere inside cinemas was different in those days. For one thing, the programmes were continuous and you could stay and see the whole programme over again, if you wanted to and some people did. There wasn't the ear-shattering music, the endless overpowering adverts and the long pauses for the sale of drinks etc. which cinemagoers have to undergo today. We went into a darkened auditorium and were shown to our seats by an usherette with a torch.

I gave my custom to a number of Brighton cinemas. There was the Regent, on the site opposite the Clock Tower, now occupied by Boots, a grand affair and its seat prices were consistent with its magnificent appearance. A cheaper and more popular cinema was the Scala, on the corner of Western Rd. and Montpelier Rd., next door to where Waitrose now stands. It changed hands and its name several times in the years that followed: 1932, the Regal; 1936, the Curzon and finally, post-war, the Classic. At one time the Scala reduced its cheapest seats to fivepence-threefarthings; an odd price but in keping with the commercial habit of the time when shops priced their materials at so many shillings and elevenpence-three farthings.

This new price gave rise to an incident with a mixture of the comic and the pathetic which could have been taken straight out of a Charlie Chaplin film. It was a Saturday afternoon and I was about twelve-years-old old at the time. By this time my system had begun to crave cinema entertainment at the week-end. So I begged the fivepence-threefarthings from my mother who more or less had to empty her purse of small change for it. I remember her turning it upside down to get the last coppers out whilst I fretted with impatience to get going, as it was a little late.

I tore down the hill to arrive, breathless, at the cinema. Imagine my feelings of alarm and disappointment when I discovered that the price had gone up again to sixpence! I was a farthing short. I was so determined to see the film that I toiled up again to the house to squeeze the extra farthing out of my mother, bolted down again and only calmed my jangling nerves when I was finally seated, breathing hard, in the all-enveloping darkness.

Later generations may well have gained the impression that the only memorable films of the period were those of Charlie Chaplin but this is far from being the case. Certainly the little man with the baggy trousers, the bowler hat, the 'tache and the cane, who walked with his toes pointed outwards, loomed large in the Hollywood output of the day. He was more of a household name than any of today's pop stars could ever be. He was the subject of endless jokes and stories; there was a comic devoted entirely to him and his antics, we copied his walk, dressed up as Charlie Chaplin at fancy-dress parties and his weepie, *The Kid*, left an indelible impression on my young mind. But there were many others, almost equally impressive, and a wide variety of films, including some great spectacles.

There was often a cartoon before the news. The earliest cartoon I remember was about Felix, the cat, and his companion and sometimes enemy, Bonzo the dog. In black and white, it always began with a human hand, drawing Felix; first, his big, pointed ears, then his huge round eyes, then his nose appearing on the screen before your eyes. His main characteristic was that he walked with his hands behind his back. There was a popular song that started: *Felix keeps on walking.*

Then came the news, either Movietone News or Pathe' Gazette, with the cockerel as its emblem. News films were much more important for us when there was no television and few people even had the wireless. It was on newsreels that I saw my first top-class cricket and football. There was a certain news-commentator voice and accentuation that was like early BBC - or even more so. There was a certain heightened anticipation about it. It had a special dramatic rise and fall that was unique, as if to say: "Watch out, something terrible, or wonderful, or funny is about to happen".

After the news there was the second feature film, a kind of fill-in before the main item. These were usually rather poor but the

80

customers demanded them; they were an essential part of the entertainment. The maiden tied across the rail track by the villain, the dashing hero snatching her from horrible death in the nick of time, her aged mother turned out in the cold, cold snow by the lecherous landlord to whom she had refused to yield; I drank it all in with an eager but quaking heart.

And the Hollywood stars, how we thrilled to them: Douglas Fairbanks. (Not Junior, that was his son) with his black wavy hair and moustache to match, the epitome of the swashbuckling daredevil, starring in The Black Pirate and The Thief of Baghdad, where the oriental costume enhanced his romantic appearance. What a man! What a boyhood hero! What food for the imagination! Rudolph Valentino, of Italian origin, with his sleek black hair parted in the middle, was the romantic Latin par excellence. It came to such a pitch that any young man known to be attractive to women might be called "a real Rudolph Valentino". He starred in: The Sheikh of Araby. The vulnerability of the romance-starved "white" woman to the charms of such a sheikh was a popular cliche' and the song in the film spoke of creeping into her tent at night. It all seemed the stuff of romance to me, even if I didn't fully understand the implications.

Among the best known women stars were Mary Pickford, "The World's Sweetheart", Pola Negri, the vamp (vanished word), with her black hair and great dark, alluring, seductive eyes, Clara Bow, the all-American "It" girl, signifying all that was thought desirable and attractive in a woman. One often heard the remark about some girl, "She's got 'It' . Greta Garbo had classic Nordic good looks and was already a highly regarded stage actress in Sweden. But it appears that she disliked the excessive publicity with which she was surrounded in Hollywood and the newshounds who were constantly pestering her. So they popularised a phrase she was supposed to have uttered constantly, " I want to be alone!" and succeeded in pinning this phrase on her as a kind of trade-mark. Certainly we all made jokes about it at the time. The power of the Press!

We had our romantics in England, too. There was Ivor Novello, with dark, wavy hair and highly sensitive, somewhat feminine features. He was an actor, a fine musician and a composer of popular sentimental songs. During the First World War, he composed, *Keep the home fires burning*, a song still sung in Old Tyme Music Hall today. Two of his successful operettas were Glamorous Nights and Kings Rhapsody which still get revived from time to time.

Noel Coward had a similar career, as actor, composer, singer, playwright and - eventually - film star. With his smooth-tongued wit and remarkable facility with words, he wrote some very witty song still popular today, and produced social and personal drama main featuring the upper classes, which perfectly encapsulated th superficial, sophisticated and amoral mood of certain circles in th Twenties and Thirties.   But he also wrote a more serious musica *Cavalcade*, which I saw in my early teens at The Regent.   The queu to get in wound round the block. A song from the play: *Twentie Century Blues*, is still a classic.   Another Englishman, Ronald Colma became a Hollywood star. With his very English voice and gentleman charm he played romantic middle-aged parts.

It wasn't only the young and handsome, however, who made name in Hollywood films. Wallace Beary was squat and ugly an often fighting drunk, playing the beer-gutted tough or the stereotyp American-Irishman.   He could also play the pathetic misfit, pleading for forgiveness.   With tears streaming down his coarse features h wrung your heart.

Talking of stereoypes, the Irish were usually cops, whilst Jews on the other hand, had to be either shopkeepers or tailors. The Irish might also be a priest and the Jewish young man perhaps a musicia or doctor. In *The Cohens and the Kellys*, the two families were constantly feuding but after much heart searching the problems ar resolved when the handsome Jewish boy marries the pretty, vivaciou Irish Colleen. Would that all enmities were so easily solved!

Hollywood Wild West films dominated children's and many adults' entertainment at the time. The children's game of Cowboy and Indians stemmed from these films. The best known star was Ton Mix, whose horse was also a star. The clean-living(!) cowboy defended "his womenfolk" against the "savage" Red Indians and, among the cowboys themselves there was always a shoot-out between the villain and the hero. The result was a foregone conclusion but that didn't prevent us from awaiting the outcome of the final showdown with bated breath. Finally, honour was satisfied and the ruggedly handsome hero was fondly embraced by the lady he'd been quarrelling with throughout the film (but *we* knew they were really in love all the time). The scenery, at least, in these films was breathtaking. Of course, nobody ever explained to us the historical realities so naturally we youngsters swallowed everything as Hollywood presented it to us.

When "The End" appeared in hazy white upon a somewhat unsteady black screen and, after standing to attention for the National Anthem, I filed out with the others into the street outside, somewhat dazzled by the street lamps, I was still filled with the emotional impact of the whole experience. It wasn't until I had entered my own home that I began to recover and get back to normality.

I saw - and heard - my first Talkie at the Tivoli, on the corner of Waterloo St. and Western Rd. Hove. It was *The Singing Fool* with Al Jolson - a real tear-jerker, in which he sang the sentimental song, *Sonny Boy*. It is the story of a widower, left alone to bring up a little son who is sickly and eventually dies.

One peculiarity of the old silent black-and-white films was the exaggerated make-up worn by the actors, characters with enormous black rings round their eyes, making the most innocent look sinister and the most serious look comical. That together with the flickering light from the projector streaming through the surrounding pitch blackness, made a visit to the cinema a deeply impressive and emotional experience for a child.

As there was no sound track, a pianist was employed to play suitable music to accompany the film. Soft and sweet for romantic moments, raucous and loud for riots and other scenes of violence, soaring and uplifting to bring inspiration where appropriate, calm ripples for scenes of quiet nature, splendid and ceremonial for scenes of pomp and circumstance, sad and mournful for the tear-jerkers. After the performance the pianist would come out from under and receive his or her due applause. It was a steady job in a profession which, even today, faces considerable periods of unemployment. Such opportunities were destroyed at a stroke when the Talkies came in.

PARKS AND RECREATION

I was well acquainted with the parks in Brighton and Hove. We played school football in Hove Park and Preston Park as well as the Recreation Ground in Dyke Rd. just behind BHASVIC (which was Direct Grant Grammar School, then). Often, after the match on Saturday morning, I stayed on with several others who were reluctant to stop kicking the football. We played on, sometimes for hours forgetting our responsibilities, like going home for dinner, for instance. Needless to say, I got into terrible trouble for this but it did not seem to cure me. There was something fascinating about a ball, some playmates, the wide open spaces especially of Preston Park. Whenever I look at the clock tower in Preston Park, these days, think of those times.

But the park which played the most significant part in my schooldays was St. Anne's Well Gardens. That was where we congregated and where I played with friends from other schools as well as my own. I looked upon it as my park. It was there that played my first cricket, betweeen two convenient trees, on which we chalked wickets, and my first football and tennis. It was surrounded by a high, wooden palisade, in those restricticve days, and shut at night.

There was an old hollow oak tree, which we used as a prop in our pirate and other games. There were also horse-chestnut trees from which we traditionally gathered conkers. The only way to do this was to throw missiles up into the branches. But it was not only that activity that incurred the wrath of the park-keepers. Almost anything we did or that seemed worth doing was apparently an excuse for them to chase us out of the park.

One was a comparatively young man, whom we named Felix (after the cartoon character) because he used to walk with his hands behind his back. So naturally we named the older man, Bonzo (Felix's sparring partner). Felix was a natural runner and we feared him most. I cannot remember if he ever caught one of us or, if he did, what punishment he meted out. But we somehow disregarded this possibility; the whole chase was part of an almost instinctive ritual and enjoyed as such, an enjoyment certainly tinged with fear.

On sunny summer evenings we used to gather there, from around 1930 when we were already well into our adolescence and the joy of sport and of the chase was undergoing subtle changes. We would listen to the band which played at weekends in the little bandstand that stood on the hill, and mingle with the crowds and try

84

to do a little hesitant flirting. The calm balmy nights, the murmur of the crowds, the music and the girls in their summer finery have all left an indelible impression on my mind.

I visited St. Anne's Well Gardens again a few years ago. The most striking difference between then and now is the openness; its high wooden fence has gone and it looks just like a bit of unfenced land but without the charm of the open countryside. The children's playground is new since my day and the bandstand has been removed. It all seems part of the neighbourhood, reflecting the sedate houses opposite, almost an extension of their front gardens.

It used to be much more self-contained, a more intimate enclosure, where fantasy could roam and we children could get on with the business of *being* children, walled in, in a world of our own. And now? Well, it isn't the St.Anne's Well Gardens of my nostalgia.

On Saturday afternoons, after playing in the morning, I always went to see Brighton and Hove Albion, when the first team was playing. It cost sixpence (2 1/2 new pence).and tuppence for a small bar of Cadbury's nut chocolate. That was my perfect weekend entertainment.

I had a friend at Varndean who got a job with an estate agent when he left school. His boss was on the management board of the Albion and my friend volunteered to sell the penny-on-the-ball tickets. This was a scheme whereby participants bought a raffle ticket for a penny and the lucky winner was given the ball used during the match. Sellers received a small commission for the sale of the tickets and saw the match for nothing. How I envied him !

At that time the Albion was in the Third Division (South) and never looked like getting out of it. The only player whose name I remember was Tommy Cook, an ex-Welsh international but well past his sell-by date. Despite their lowly position and the mediocre level of play, it was always fascinating to watch professionals, if only to observe the basic footballing skills such as trapping the ball and moving forward at the same time, or taking the ball on the chest or in the midriff, with arms stiffly by the sides to form a kind of receiving pad. Even the way they kicked the ball was instructive. We liked to shout out encouragements and even permitted ourselves facetious insults like: "'e's unsteady on 'is pins". They wore long, baggy shorts which might seem comical, today.

I was told that they were all to be found carousing in a local pub on Saturday evening, and thus taking little heed of physical fitness. They certainly never seemed to advance much above the middle of the table, though I think they once beat Portsmouth when they got a little further than usual in the Cup competition.

I never once attended a county cricket match, but was an avid Sussex supporter, nonetheless, read the results, batting and bowling performances, with great interest, was elated when they won and keenly disappointed when they lost. They had some fine players in those days. Perhaps the most famous was Maurice Tate, the medium-paced bowler, who was a permanent fixture in the England and MCC sides, for years. He was a biggish, thick-set man, with a red face; a real Farmer Giles type in appearance and tremendously popular with the public. Then there was the Gilligan family, A.E.R. being Sussex captain and a great all-rounder.

Perhaps their most famous batsman, who was also a brilliant fielder, was Duleepsinghi, related to the equally famous Ranjitsinghi (before my time). " Duleep" was from a wealthy and, I believe, aristocratic family in India; one of many such, sent to study at English Public Schools in order, presumably, to turn them into acceptable members of upper class English society.

There were many other gifted players in the county side. One nationally known figure was "Titch"Cornford, the wicketkeeper, who also played some time for England and was pretty handy with the bat, too. Sussex were always an attractive and successful side, though they never won the county championship . It was all Yorkshire and Surrey, especially Yorkshire, who were in the limelight, often won the championship and had many internationally famous players.

The interesting thing was, however, that Yorkshire were several times defeated by Sussex who, nonetheless, finished lower down the table. All this information was gleaned at second hand. I sucked up every piece of news I could, about the club and its players from friends, including those adults who attended matches, as well as from newspaper reports and news films at the cinema.

I also followed the English team in its struggles with the Australians for the Ashes. Here, it was Jack Hobbs and Herbert Sutcliffe (Surrey and Yorkshire again) who were our great heroes. It was some sort of disaster if they didn't make a century opening stand, at least. Each was expected to score an individual century, anyway. Other great names that stirred our schoolboy hearts were Wally Hammond, the Gloucester all-rounder, Jardine, a batsman who, I believe, captained Warwickshire, Strudwick, the automatic choice for wicketkeeper, with our Cornford as his stand-in, and Larwood, of Notts, the "bodyline" bowler.

Towering above them all, however, was the Australian star batsman, the mighty Don Bradman to whom, so it seemed to me, centuries were commonplace and only his double and treble centuries were worth a mention. When Larwood toured Australia, spreading fear and anger among the batsmen, who accused him of terror tactics, Bradman showed them just how to deal with that or any other sort of bowling by knocking his bowling all over the ground. But then - he was Bradman!

One event, connected with cricket, which caused great excitement in the town, took place in front of the new aquarium during a test match. A huge white screen was erected in front of the entrance. It towered over the whole area and was supported by some sort of high platform. It could be seen quite clearly from every part of the Old Steine, from the Palace Pier entrance and from the Royal Albion corner. An oval cricket pitch was represented on it.

The creases at each end of the pitch were easily visible. The ball was represented by a large, movable red spot. As the ball was bowled, it was shown to move and when it was struck it moved again to indicate its line of travel. The score was clearly displayed at the bottom and instantly changed, as required. The names of all the players were given on each side of the oval. Both above and below the whole thing, was the name of the sponsors in large letters: **Johnnie Walker** and the slogan: *1820 NOT OUT.*

The area now occupied by the roundabout was packed solid. We could hardly move. There was great jollity and cameraderie amongst the crowd and, when someone started community singing, we all joined in lustily. Normally, I feel quite embarrassed about my tunelessness in public but, in a crowd like that, I felt quite safe. I remember bawling out John Brown's Body, at the top of my voice, along with everybody else and laughing and joking with my neighbours. I even had the temerity to make up new witty words to the song which, surprisingly, were appreciated by those around me. Quite a comic, the boy!

Overleaf: *The Johnnie Walker Scoreboard*

87

TWO BRIEF INTERLUDES

In 1928, at the beginning of the summer term, the whole family moved to Yarmouth for a short spell. My father had decided to try East Anglia, as business was getting bad in Brighton. Apart from all the other upheavals, there was also the question of finding places at local schools. I remember some of the lessons and two of the teachers at the school I went to. One of these was a middle-aged man of somewhat stocky build, who was form master and English teacher.

He soon cottoned on to my strengths and weaknesses. Fortunately for me he rapidly discoverd that the messy, blotty essays were worth deciphering. And he also commended my reading. Sure enough, just as at Christ Church, I was deputed to act as class "voice" when anything had to be read aloud. Is it excusable human nature that I remember these positive reactions rather than the negative ones?

The other man was a young student teacher from the local college. He was a P.T. specialist and we got on rather well. I managed to con him into believing that I was a talented cricketer by telling him the truth - as far as it went - that I had played for the school team in Brighton. What I omitted to say was that there wasn't a serious schools' cricket league in Brighton and that, anyway, in the rare inter-school matches, I did not do very well and was only included because there were so few senior boys in the school and I was an automatic choice because I looked tough!

When it came to an actual match, in Yarmouth, I was put in at number 4 but did not distinguish myself. I seem to remember getting a few runs before swiping blindly at a fairly easy ball and being bowled. That was the end of my cricketing career at the Yarmouth school. They evidently took their cricket much more seriously than we did in Brighton. I also remember seeing the young man, who was slim, tall and athletic, playing cricket for his college. Standing at the gates to the college which stood in its own grounds, I watched him and his team from afar. Their white-flannelled magnificence placed them far beyond my world.

Whilst we were in Yarmouth, several members of the family came to visit us, Uncle Harry and Auntie Polly and their eldest daughter Malka, from Birmingham and two of the Schmidts from London. Other memories of Yarmouth are the various entertainers that proliferated along the sandy beach. One in particular was a most peculiar marionette show, on a tiny stage, about half the height of a Punch-and-Judy show. The showman's head poked through a hole in the curtain and appeared to be the head of the little velvet-suited marionette, in front of the curtain. Little sticks also poked through the curtain and were attached to the back of the marionette's hands and feet.

The showman manipulated these to make the hands and arms move, whilst he sang various children's hit songs of the period. The one that stands out in my mind is:

The Hip-hip-hip-opotamus,
He can do more than the lot of us,
He can stay, so they say,
Underneath the water for half a day;
The Hip-hip-hip-opotamus,
Is a clever feller in his way,
But the whole bally lot of us,
Can beat the hipopotamus,
He can't hip-hip-hooray!

And we all sang along. Another popular ditty of the day was *Barney Google (with his goo-goo-googly eyes!)* Note the repetitive factor, common to both songs.

One result of our term out, in Yarmouth, was that when we returned we discovered that the Intermediate School had been set up for those pupils who had failed the "schol" but were considered able to benefit from a somewhat more specialised education than that provided by the Elementary School. It meant that they had an opportunity to sit the Matric exam (equivalent of "O" Levels) and thus qualify for further or higher education.

Our Mr. Smith was on the staff there when it started. We met him, by chance, one day, outside the Regent Cinema, opposite the Clock Tower. He button-holed my parents and offered to get me in to his school, if they so desired. There was a small fee. My father declined. I assume he wanted me to start work as soon as possible, or felt he could not afford the fee or, perhaps, had no confidence in my academic ability.

Whatever the reason, I lost my chance to advance to higher education in normal progression, i.e. straight from school to college. That I managed to get a university degree by quite another route, much later in life, is another story. Incidentally, the Intermediate had the strongest football team of any school in Brighton.

The second interlude was one summer, when the whole family went to live in a farmer's house in a small village near Hurstpierpoint. I was probably about eleven years old at the time. The reason for the visit may have been that I was getting over some illness or perhaps my father had some work in the area.

I have retained but a few brief images of our stay there. On one occasion I was asked to take a bottle of cold tea to the farmer, at midday, who was out working in the fields. My route took me through a grassy path between two fields, high with crops. It was a strange, even eerie, feeling. What should have been a huge silence was, instead, filled with all the mysterious noises of the countryside - mysterious, that is, to a townee like me.

Above the occasional sighing of a slight warm breeze that stirred the ears of wheat, there were several other noises, some of which sounded quite sinister and sent shivers of apprehension through my limbs. At every twig that cracked or leaf that stirred, I thought of foxes or other wild things - even snakes. My steps became more hurried and I was greatly relieved to arrive at my destination and find the farmer and his son, lying down in the shelter of a hedge, beginning to munch their bread and cheese.

They were no doubt equally pleased to see me, carrying the precious thirst-quencher. After I had shared their lunch and watched them using the reaping-and-binding machine, the son accompanied me back to the house. His company so reassured me that the nervousness of the earlier journey completely vanished.

Another memory of that holiday was of playing cricket for the village team. I was younger than the rest of the team but it was part of their kindness to make me feel at home and part of the village life. I can't remember my batting performance but I do remember fielding. By remarkable good luck, I actually hit the stumps with a direct throw when throwing in. Although the umpire judged the running batsman not out, I felt pretty pleased with myself.

After the match, there was a wonderful farmhouse tea in the garden of the cricket-green pub, with delicious strawberries and cream. For some reason, when the rest of the family left for home, I remained behind for a few days. During this period, I ate with the host family and was wonderfully well looked after.

One evening at dinner someone sneezed. "Good health!" cried everyone, except me. I said:"Tsugesunt!" and explained that it meant the same thing - in Yiddish. I then endeavoured to get them to pronounce it properly. They found the "ts" difficult and we all collapsed in laughter at their attempts. I reminded them that many English words have this same sound, e.g. cats, mats etc. I mention the incident because it was an early example of my efforts (subsequently professional) to teach foreign languages.

On another occasion I was watching the farmer drive the cattle home, one sunny, summer evening. He was walking behind them and occasionally shouting encouragement to them to hurry along. I thought I'd help a little by adding my voice to his. I noticed that they avoided me as far as possible by hugging the railed fence as they passed me in single file. I was puzzled by this until he told me that, far from helping, I was frightening them to death! But, kind man that he was, he didn't seem to mind.

LIFE IN BRIGHTON IN THE TWENTIES

Nothing seemed to change in Brighton during my schooldays. Western Rd. in 1930, when I left school, looked to my youthful eyes much as it had looked when we arrived nearly ten years earlier. One important new building that went up in the late Twenties was Varndean Girls' School "on the edge of the Downs", to which my youngest sister, who now preferred to be called Ethel, had won the scholarship in 1928. The boys' Secondary School was built on the opposite prominence a little later.

There were a few other memorable happenings that stand out. One was the beating of the bounds. This is an ancient, traditional ceremony that apparently used to take place when a town got new boundaries, as Brighton did on April 1st, 1928, following the 1927 Brighton Corporation Act. Schools were given a holiday and the whole of the new boundary was lined by schoolchildren furnished with sticks. At a given signal, we all started hitting the road or pavement with these sticks. The excitement mounted and somehow the idea got around that people were to be bumped. I was the first!

Many pairs of hands grabbed me, lifted me off my feet horizontally, sat me on the pavement with no great delicacy and then lifted me up again, the process being repeated several times. After me, other victims were sought. Eventually, believe it or not, we gave the same treatment to the Headmaster. He was a prim and proper man but could do little to prevent it.

Remembrance Day was a far more solemn and impressive occasion than it is today. It was always held on 11th November: the eleventh hour of the eleventh day of the eleventh month. Poppies of different size and price were sold in all schools. Penny ones were small and simple; those with three layers of leaves cost threepence; sixpenny ones were more lavish still. Gorgeously ostentatious poppies, usually bought by teachers only, could be obtained for a shilling.

At eleven o'clock, precisely, a hooter went and everything stopped for two minutes silence, to remember the dead. There was a deathly hush throughout the town. It was as though the whole world stood still. The seconds ticked away as I recalled the inscription I had seen on a war memorial: "In the morning and at the going down of the sun - we shall remember them!" At the sound of another hooter, noisy normality returned. Quite impressive. For a moment we had been confronted with the obscenity of millions of young lives lost: someone's brother, father, husband, son.

A tremendous stir was caused by the visit of the Prince of Wales, later to be Edward VII and, later still after marrying Mrs. Simpson, the Duke of Windsor. I was taken to Preston Park by Mr. Landon, our lodger from the basement flat. By the time we got there the gates were shut; I don't know why.

"Teddy" was extremely popular. As we stood there, eager but disappointed, the royal entourage arrived at the gate and there was the hero, the epitome of youthful charm, smiling his boyish smile at the packed crowd. His nonchalant style of dress, his debonair manner, all endeared him to the common people. And I couldn't help noticing that Mr. Landon, an Ulstertman of impeccable Unionist sentiments, was glowing with pride.

One other activity that aroused great interest in the town was the fact that some Channel swimmers did their training here. The most famous one was Jabez Wolfe. I often saw his rotund little figure padding down the beach for a practice swim, pushing into the water and then gradually disappearing from view as he swam towards the horizon. I don't know if he ever actually made it across to France.

It was at this time, also, that the News Chronicle ran a publicity stunt. They printed a very inadequate photograph of part of a man's face, shaded by his hat. He was called Lobby Ludd. He was coming to Brighton to mingle with the crowd. There was a cash prize for the first person to identify him. You had to go up to him and boldly declare: "You are Mr. Lobby Ludd. I claim the News Chronicle £5 prize. "

The famous saucy postcards also seem to epitomise the Brighton of the Twenties. Example: A fat man with a huge belly, in a swimming costume, is unable to see that, beneath the rounded curve stands a little boy. Caption: "Has anyone here seen my little Willy?" The shops that sold them also sold Brighton rock. As to the "What-the-butler-saw" machines, I thought them a waste of time and money.

That there were fewer cars in those days does not mean that there were no traffic problems. The bottom of Preston St. was something of a bottleneck. In order to deal with the problem they installed a kind of novel, mechanical traffic control there, a forerunner of traffic lights. It was a signpost that could be moved up and down by remote control. The warning sign was attached to a fixed metal pole on the edge of the left-hand pavement, at the bottom of the street. It contained one word: STOP, in black on white. It dropped into a horizontal position to halt the traffic. I don't know when this contraption was removed to make way for our modern system.

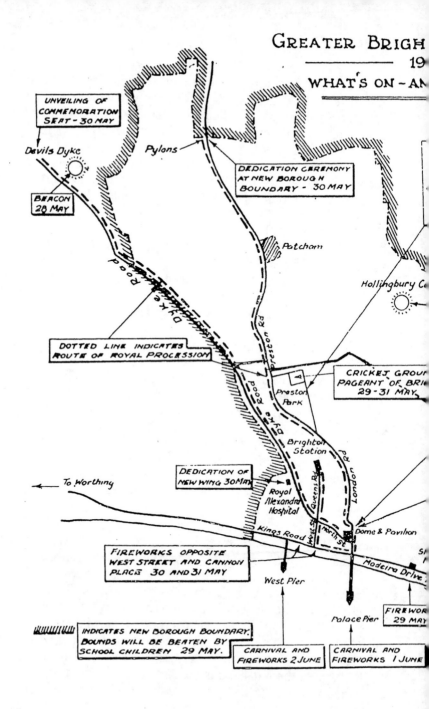

UNVEILING OF COMMEMORATION SEAT - 30 MAY

Devils Dyke

Pylons

BEACON 28 MAY

DEDICATION CEREMONY AT NEW BOROUGH BOUNDARY - 30 MAY

DYKE ROAD

Patcham

Hollingbury C

DOTTED LINE INDICATES ROUTE OF ROYAL PROCESSION

Preston Rd

CRICKET GROUN PAGEANT OF BRI 29 - 31 MAY.

DYKE ROAD

Preston Park

Brighton Station

DEDICATION OF NEW WING 30 MAY

To Worthing

Royal Alexandra Hospital

London Rd

West St

Queens Rd

North St

Dome & Pavilion

Kings Road

FIREWORKS OPPOSITE WEST STREET AND CANNON PLACE 30 AND 31 MAY.

Madeira Drive

SF

West Pier

FIREWOR 29 MAY

INDICATES NEW BOROUGH BOUNDARY. BOUNDS WILL BE BEATEN BY SCHOOL CHILDREN 29 MAY.

Palace Pier

CARNIVAL AND FIREWORKS 2 JUNE

CARNIVAL AND FIREWORKS 1 JUNE

Celebrations

ERE - AT A GLANCE

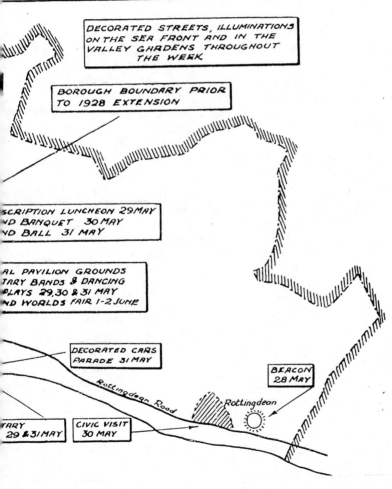

OUTS & GIRL GUIDES DISPLAY - 29 MAY
T & FIRE BRIGADE DISPLAY - 29, 30 & 31 MAY
SHOW, GYMKHANA & MILITARY.
 TOURNAMENT 30-31 MAY
Y BANDS, DANCING & FIREWORKS
 30-31 MAY
MATCH - NEW ZEALAND V. SUSSEX 31 MAY
 VISITORS V. BRIGHTON 1 JUNE

DECORATED STREETS, ILLUMINATIONS
ON THE SEA FRONT AND IN THE
VALLEY GARDENS THROUGHOUT
THE WEEK

BOROUGH BOUNDARY PRIOR
TO 1928 EXTENSION

SCRIPTION LUNCHEON 29 MAY
ND BANQUET 30 MAY
ND BALL 31 MAY

AL PAVILION GROUNDS
TARY BANDS & DANCING
PLAYS 29, 30 & 31 MAY
ND WORLDS FAIR 1-2 JUNE

DECORATED CARS
PARADE 31 MAY

BEACON
28 MAY

Rottingdean Road

Rottingdean

TARY
29 & 31 MAY

CIVIC VISIT
30 MAY

Two great names of those days stand out in my mind. First there was Malcolm Campbell, the motor speed fanatic. He started his spectacular attacks on the world land speed record in 1924. From then on, at regular intervals, we were regaled with stories and films of his successive (and successful) attempts to better his own previous record. I drank in the danger and trembled every time I saw a film of his racing car rashly hurtling along the salt flats.

The other great name lauded, literally, to the skies was Amy Johnson, the first woman to fly solo to Australia - in a tiny little aircraft. At one point, she flew over Brighton and we all gazed constantly up at the sky on the day it was supposed to happen. Later she visited Elm Grove School. They even made up a song about her. *Amy, wonderful Amy, we're proud of the way you flew.* It was a time of intense pressure for the British to be the best at everything. In our school atlases we saw the numerous areas coloured red, denoting our empire, "upon which the sun never sets" and of which, it was continually stressed, we should all feel proud.

Another great event of the time was the building of the new aquarium, later changed into a dolphinarium and now transformed into the Sea Life Centre. The old building had closed down in 1927 for modernisation. Its famous clock tower was demolished, causing much heartache. The new, resplendent, whiter than white structure arose, completed in 1929 and ceremoniously re-opened by the Duchess of York (present Queen Mother) on 12th June.

Some people regarded it as a monstrosity and mourned the passing of the old aquarium. But the powers that be were convinced that it was a great new attraction for the town. Most of us children had hardly noticed this momentous transformation until Wag decided to hold a debate on the subject, in one of our class meetings.

The motion was: "That the new aquarium is a white elephant" - a new expression for me. In the debate we contrived some more or less witty word play and verbal fencing which these debates gave us ample opportunity to practise. There were some attempts, for example, at schoolboy humour about elephants and fish. At any rate, the debate brought this great civic enterprise to our attention. Though I suppose we should have noticed it eventually.

I was not fully aware of what life was like in some other areas. Whitehawk was more or less foreign territory to me and Moulsecoomb was a separate estate that we passed through on our way out of Brighton on some country hike. However, despite having a number of children at the school who were slightly better off, there were several boys who were obviously in poor circumstances, thin, small and even stunted in growth. No wonder I was regarded as a fatty.

Some of the boys wore ragged clothing. One in particular, with whom I was quite friendly, had his shirt-tail sticking out of the seat of his trousers. The Head or the class teacher would, from time to time, appeal for second-hand clothing from those who appeared more affluent. I remember my mother responding to this request by giving one of my jackets A small boy wore it as a coat for quite a considerable time. I was reminded of this, a year or so later when Wag wanted to make a further request on the boy's behalf. These straitened conditions had no immediate conscious efffect on my social outlook but their effects sank in and influenced me later.

Most of the friends I have mentioned were in a similar position to myself. Some were poorer; some were better off if their fathers had a secure job in a recognised trade or profession, or who were independent businessmen, like Ernie's, who owned a pub. But the social circumstances of my friends' families never seemed to affect our relationship.

I was always keenly aware that our middle-class "front" was just that - a front. I usually had one good suit, made by Uncle Sholem, in Birmingham, but could never dress fashionably or look really smart and I seldom had more than one pair of shoes. I think this had a decided effect on my self esteem. We got no regular pocket money, only the occasional handout, if Dad was feeling flush or if some special occasion demanded it. I often had to plead with my mother to give me sixpence to go to the pictures. That is why I came to rely on my earnings on the Little Stockbroker.

I suppose things got much worse for most people from 1929 onwards, after the American stock market collapse. But I can remember no such clear cut change in circumstances, in my family or among my friends. I know that my mother became increasingly worried about money matters. How well I recall her distress when, at the doctor's, she had to dig deep into her purse to pay him his fee and for the medicines at the chemist's. It may sound overdramatised, but the look on her face tugged at my heartstrings.

At the hospital you had to be interviewed by the Lady Almoner who probed into your financial circumstances and made you feel terribly demeaned. Phrases like: "Surely you could afford more than that, Mrs.Goldman", still stick in the gullet. In those days, you paid your way or it was charity and people who appeared respectable were just unable to "lower themselves" for that. Victorian values with a vengeance!

THE WORLD OF WORK

Schooldays seemed to go on for ever but at last my great leaving day arrived, some weeks before my fourteenth birthday, at the end of the summer term, 1930. I can remember no special gesture from Wag to say goodbye, but I believe the school signified they would be pleased to see me back any time I cared to visit. Apparently the school provided many Western Rd. stores with apprentices and I went for an interview at Chipperfied and Butler, a drapery store a few doors from the Midland Bank near the top of Preston St. Dyas now occupy the site. They wanted a school leaver to train as an assistant.

They offered me half-a-crown a week (less than £5 at today's values) for the first year, as a concession, after my father had been to see them and doubled it to five shillings (25 p.) for the second year. Apprentices were not really entitled to any wages at all, they said, because they were giving you a training! All assistants - even those on half-a-crown a week - had to wear white shirts and detached stiff white collars, held in place by studs back and front, giving rise to sore skin especially behind the back stud. The suit had to be a respectable dark colour, as did the shoes and the tie.

C.and B. was a somewhat smaller edition of, say, Hanningtons or Vokins and somewhere in between the two as to the class of goods (and customers) it served. They sold materials for ladies' dresses - a large department this - and also haberdashery and linens, all on the ground floor. Ladies' clothing was upstairs

In the basement we had the soft furnishing department, to which I was assigned. We sold curtaining and upholstery materials, including net curtains, cushions, footstools, carpets, blankets and down quilts - genuine eiderdowns were very expensive and had to be ordered. And many and varied were the skills I had to acquire. Salesmanship seemed to come naturally but the more practical tasks needed careful explanation and practice.

The departmental hierarchy consisted of the buyer, a kind of generalissimo, who in our case ruled over two departments - ours and the linens. Next came the first sales. This was the person who had first crack of the whip when a customer appeared. Since we got a small commission on every item we sold, these seniority rights were of great importance. Then there was the second sales; in our department this was a young lady of about 30, who served if the first sales was occupied. I can remember that she wore a gorgeous engagement ring. As there were no others in our department, I came next. These relativities were jealously defended. Woe betide a junior who served a customer when their senior was available!

I discovered the truth of this one day when the other two were out of sight somewhere and a chap from another department brought down a customer and asked me to serve her. She turned out to be Wilhemina Stitch, a well known journalist on the Daily Sketch, I think. She ordered a genuine eiderdown - the only one that was ever sold whilst I was there - that was very expensive, seven pounds (about £200 by today's reckoning). You can imagine the fury of my two superiors when they found out.

There was also a floorwalker, who was there to help the customers in various different ways. He directed them to the department they required, acted as a general source of information and lent an aura, on the one hand, of magnificence and, on the other, of felicitous concern for their welfare. He was always flawlesly dressed in frock-coat and tails.

Our buyer was a Mr. Smith, a tall, broad-shouldered man with an abstracted air, a stooping shoulder and a slanted smile. We did not see him very often. My real boss was the first sales, a Mr. R... who was about forty. He had two bug teeth in front and tended to splutter at the mouth. You kept out of reach when he was speaking at speed.

He had gingerish, brushed-back hair, thinning and greying at the temples. Like my father, he had received a slight wound whilst on service. He had been holding on to one of the shoulder straps of his pack when the flash from an exploding shell struck his right hand. As a result, the fingers remained stiff and set in a curled position. He overcame this disability remarkably well, considering he was having to handle material all day long.

He was pleasant and friendly except when you got him on politics which, in my inexperience, I sometimes foolishly did. I was in the first flush of youthful indignation at the wrongs of society and enthusiasm for sweeping them aside, though I may have been somewhat vague about what the remedies might be. Unemployment was the most frequent bone of contention. He saw the unemployed as a bunch of work-shy layabouts ("A spot of army discipline would do 'em good!"). I challenged this with the knee-jerk reaction of the young. I *knew* it was "the system" that created unemployment.

"There are millions of people hungry and cold for want of food, clothing and shelter," I said. "There are 3 million unemployed. Why can't they be put to work supplying those needs?" As soon as the atmosphere became charged and I could see he was getting worked up, I shut up like a clam and, in general, we got on very well and I certainly learnt a lot from him much of which is still useful to me.

He taught me the cost-price code, which was LD BROUGHAM, each letter representing a number from 1 to 0. The profit margin was 33 1/3% "on returns", i.e. 50% on the cost price. It was important to know all this at sales times, when reductions were in the offing. He also taught me a few tricks which come in handy sometimes. Firstly, how to run down a flight of stairs at speed, by turning the toes outwards (à la Charlie Chaplin) to maintain balance. Secondly, how to open a new ball of string, by winkling out the end of the string from the aperture in the centre. It still annoys me to see people trying to open one up from the outside and destroying the whole ball in the process. The third trick was how to break off a length of string by winding it round the middle finger at the desired breaking point and snapping it down with a jerk. It worked !

The first real drapery skill I had to learn was to roll or unroll the bales of cloth. Each end has to be absolutely straight and flat, at right angles to the width of the roll. Unrolling needs skill, too. A small amount may be unrolled to show it to a customer or many yards, when a purchase has been made. This must be done along the counter, keeping the volume of material in an orderly pile on top of it, no dropping parts of it on the floor or getting it tangled in a confused heap.

For measuring there was a brass yardstick affixed to the edge of the counter. You grasped the edge of the material between forefinger and thumb, placing the right hand grasping the end of the cloth on the beginning of the measure. Letting the cloth slip through the forefinger and thumb of your left hand, you then slid the left hand holding the cloth across to the end of the measure, thus measuring one yard of material. This process was continued until the required amount had been measured. A detached yardstick could also be used.

Then there is the cutting. The eye must be able to judge a straight line. Scissors or shears must be kept sharp so as not to damage the material. Special attention must be paid when there is a pattern. Sometimes the pattern is not true, or the material is twisted. Net curtaining is especially difficult. Folding the material before packing also presents problems. The edge is grasped again but this time held high in front of you and lifted, alternately right and left until the end. It is then folded into a neat rectangle, ready for packing.

The various types of material have to be known by name and their qualities and suitability for various uses thoroughly understood. There were reps and artificial silks, twill, sub-silk (containing little thick threads to break up the evenness of the surface), linen, various types of cotton stuff, cretonnes, printed, patterned or plain material and so on. There was also the question of colour and, sometimes, the necessity of matching the customer's own material.

I had to learn the myriad tones and shades that manufacturers of textiles were producing and often changing. Green was not just light or dark but reseda, leaf green, jade, etc. And there was a similar multiplicity of shades for all the other colours. It wasn't just that a customer might want an exact colour but that many customers didn't know what they wanted and the assistant had to be an adviser on all aspects of the goods he was selling. And all that for half-a-crown a week!

Apart from measuring and cutting off the required amount, care had to be taken not to damage especially delicate or expensive material, but to fold it correctly. What was not required had to be re-rolled, returned to the exactly correct place on the shelf or elsewhere, and the customer's purchase had to be neatly packed. To this day, I am the family parcel-packer and material-cutter and folder. I am also the expert curtain hooker and hanger because these skills, once learnt, are never forgotten.

Mr.R... addressed the customers in an exaggerated patrician accent and I, nothing loth, followed suit. There were two reasons for this. Firstly, several of the staff were from a middle class background and as, in those days, accent mattered, it wouldn't do to be heard using an "inferior" one. One had to keep up with the Jones's. But perhaps this was even more true when it came to the customers. If they spoke that way you had to match them. If they didn't, your assumed upper-class accent somehow gave you the edge, in a situation where the customer was "always right".

For me, with my love of acting and putting on various voices, as well as airs and graces, the whole thing came quite naturally. The result was that I almost completely lost my Brighton accent, though it peeps through at times. I also acquired the manners and poses of a shop assistant, by slavishly copying Mr.R.....A whole host of trite phrases tripped off the tongue as a substitute for real conversation.

I had been at the firm for about a year, when a somewhat dramatic occurence took place. One day Mr.R.... did not turn up and an air of mystery pervaded the department. Whispering groups containing people from other departments made me very inquisitive indeed. Finally, I heard the full story. A plain-clothes detective had been into the department one afternoon when the first hand was on his own and made a purchase. This purchase was apparently not recorded in the little receipt book which all salespeople had. And, it turned out, he had been doing this for quite a time and on an increasing scale and pocketing the money, himself.

The remark of the young lady assistant, the one with the engagement ring - but an odd grasp of English - sticks in my mind. " I never suspicioned anything!" she said. After Mr. R...'s departure, she became the first sales and my new boss. She was quite friendly but she had a habit of hounding me whenever I didn't appear to be doing anything. One of the great bugbears in such stores was that you were always supposed to be "doing something", even when there was nothing to do. Eventually I developed a kind of defence mechanism; I always carried a duster or some other stage prop and would be working away assiduously when she wanted to know what I was doing.

After a year, I was transferred to the Linen Department, upstairs. There, the first hand was a very likeable youngish man, a Mr.Penn (the one who had been involved in the eiderdown rumpus). He had a friendly, brisk manner, wore rimless glasses and was quite a ladies' man. He had a good singing voice and was a member of the local amateur operatic society which, at that time, was producing *The Pirates of Penzance*, in which he was a member of the chorus. He was always immaculately dressed and spoke in a soft melodious voice, so that the atmosphere in that department was much more relaxed..

When we were not busy, he would come and tell me about his past experiences and how he himself started in the trade. Apparently his first boss pretended to be a tyrant in order to instil a sense of discipline in him, but in reality had a heart of gold. The items we sold there were towels, sheets, pillow-cases, and materials for sheets and sleeping suits such as Wincyette. At Christmas, they decided to decorate the store with arches in front of the counters as though we were selling in an arcade. I was deputed to help the window-dresser to make these false fronts, in a nearby building which was used as a workshop.

This young man was tall, with fair wavy hair and, as I later discovered, quite a heart-throb. He was very artistic but also very impulsive and didn't suffer fools gladly. Unfortunately, practical work of this kind was not my forte. So, although we started off on a very friendly basis - he told me to call him by his first name, which was rather unusual in those days - it wasn't long before he came up against what he must have thought of as my deliberate obtuseness and he began to get very unpleasant.

To cut the unhappy story short, I was glad to get back behind the counter with friendly Mr. Penn. This rather souring experience did not, however, stop me explaining to the customers just how the rather impressive decorations had been made and hinting at my involvement in the process. There was a peculiar fascination in letting the customers into little secrets and drawing them a little closer into the world behind the counter.

In general, the relationship with the customers was a special one. It was also an education to observe their little peculiarities and foibles. I discoverd that the hard sell was not within my nature. I could only lead them gently to a purchase. When that didn't work I was at something of a loss. And here I should mention that if a customer "swapped" you (walked out without buying) you could get into trouble if your superior found out. In fact, if there was a danger of losing a sale, you were supposed to call the first hand to see if they could prevent that happening.

The boss of the firm was a Mr. Butler. Chipperfield was either dead, or "sleeping" or had been bought out. Mr. Butler was a thin, nervous, white-haired man, with pince-nez glasses and a very serious, preoccupied air. He always wore dark suits, a white shirt and a bow tie. His office was upstairs and we did not see a great deal of him. He left the running of the store to his departmental managers. When I entered the firm, he was just introducing his son to the business, whom we had to address as Mr.John. This young man was in his middle twenties, I suppose. He was tall and slim, with a faint moustache, and wore a fashionably-cut pale grey suit and, like his father, sported a bow-tie. He had recently become engaged and we all saw his bride-to-be and, if I remember rightly, contributed to a present.

By great co-incidence, a few years ago, I was involved in a project to research pre-war retail trade in Brighton and the young researchers told me that they had been in touch with this "young" Mr.Butler. I wrote to him and received no reply for some time. Sadly, some months later, his son wrote telling me that his father had died. I suppose he must have been in his late eighties.

During the summer months, when the weather was suitable, I used to go down to the beach during my lunch hour and erect the tent. I would go in for a swim and wash away the dust and stress of the shop. All the tensions, worries, noise and talk would recede into the background and it was just me and the sea, with the waves gently rocking me to and fro as I floated, trod water, lazily swam out some distance from the shore and let the ocean take care of me.

Often, at that time of day, the beach was almost deserted. At an agreed time, my mother would appear with a steaming hot meal for me which she had carried down from the house. I can distinctly remember steak and chips, for instance. I demolished those meals with an appetite made more voracious by the swimming and returned to work refreshed and invigorated.

A favourite occupation during lunch breaks was playing cards in the tiny staff-room. Some of the older members of staff introduced me to poker and I got quite hooked on it. Fortunately they rarely played for money and, even when they did, it was for very small stakes. They played solo, too, a game with which I was already familiar since we played it at home. I also learnt shove-ha'penny and became quite proficient at it. Somehow, the feel of the coin as I hit it with the heel of my thumb gave me considerable satisfaction. I may not, in general, have been much of a sportsman but - I excelled at shove-ha'penny.

Another activity was playing football for a Western Rd. Traders side composed of youngsters working in shops and offices in the area. The fiance' of one of the young ladies working at C. and B. was a footballer of some ability and he asked around for volunteers for a match against a team from somewhere in Sussex. The little practice we had in an open field just in front of the racecourse was hardly sufficient against a team that trained regularly.

Despite this, we all turned up on the appointed day, kitted out for the game. I was wearing a pair of boots too tight for me and with a nail sticking up inside. My shorts, too, were so thin they were in danger of tearing at any moment. In fact, I was still using the kit I wore at school. I do not remember a great deal of the match. I was probably out of practice - I hadn't played since I'd left school - and most of the others were older than me. I did get a couple of good kicks at the ball on that very windy pitch and fed one of our forwards with a pass from which he nearly scored. Then disaster struck, my shorts tore in an awkward place. Fortunately one of the others had a pair of tight bathing trunks he could lend me to go underneath, so my modesty was protected. We lost, but they provided us with an excellent tea afterwards.

POLITICAL AWARENESS

My mother always claimed that it was she who influenced my political orientation - and who am I to argue? It seems that, on Sunday mornings, we fell to discussing the world and its woes. She spoke of her own experiences in Russia and on the possibilities of a better, fairer world. A compassionate and emotional person, she empathised with the suffering and the downtrodden.

I, too, had deeply emotional feelings of perceived injustices which led to the adoption of a position on the Left at an early age. But there was an added factor that I am very conscious of, namely, that several of my closest friends were already commited to "the cause". The two I am mostly thinking of were Bob and Roy.

They and a few like-minded youngsters in their mid teens had formed a youth branch of the Independant Labour Party, known as The Guild of Youth. It had its premises in a building half way up Elm Grove. The space behind the shop window was now a small hall. There was also a meeting room upstairs as well as some leisure facilities, including a billiard table. A lot of our schoolfriends used to turn up there, mainly to social events. I particularly remember Roy's elder brother, Gordon, a handsome young man with crisp, dark, curly hair smoothed down from the temple and a classic profile. There were a lot of girls there, too, and that aded to the interest and excitement.

I was easily persuaded to join the Guild, though I cannot remember ever paying any dues. We were a very earnest crowd and the discussions were long and heated, if not always well-informed. We also knew how to enjoy ourselves both indoors and out. There were dances and socials and we continued the practice of rambles over the Downs, to which Wag had introduced us. Refreshments were also available at the hall and I began to be drawn into a new social milieu, all tied up with a Left-wing political perspective, the naivete of inexperienced youth being no barrier to an introduction to serious adult perceptions. Indeed, it was a positive advantage as we were able to discuss without the restraints and cautions of age.

On one occasion an adult member of the ILP, came to talk to us. He adopted a somewhat schoolmasterly approach. Having obviously sized us up, he started by saying that "although you are all well fed and clothed, I am sure you know that there are many, even in prosperous England, who are not." And then he went on to preach the socialist message, which I could later recite by heart, that in a just society nature's provisions would be available to all and no man(sic) would exploit his neighbour. Looking round at the world today, this still remains a worthwhile vision - a hope for mankind.

One evening in 1930, a jolly, bouncy, rather bumptious and very confident young man who, I was told, was an estate agent, came to report to us on his recent visit to the Soviet Union. He spoke with some enthusiasm of what he had seen and heard. It was his second visit, as he'd been there some years earlier, and this time, he said, they seemed much more confident of their future, "more cock-a-hoop" was the expression he used. And his name? Lewis (later Lord) Cohen. When he had finished, we questioned him closely.

I was feeling particularly critical and, because of what my grandfather had told us in his letters, I felt I had some first-hand information to communicate. My question was not taken too seriously although I cannot remember the answer, only that I was rather put off by it. On the way home with Roy, I asked him about the Soviet Union and what "our attitude" towards it was."We are socialists," he said. "And what is the difference between communism and socialism?", I asked. How many times in later life have I been asked to reply to that same question! His reply was prompt: "Socialism is constructive; communism is destructive," he proclaimed, knowingly.

That many of my schoolfriends and I were, at the very least, prepared to question the generally accepted assumptions of the time strengthens my belief that Wag's influence was also partly responsible for our attitude of mind. I have already referred to his iconoclastic attitude and how he introduced us to Shaw and Wells. He always insisted on asking "Why?" or "How do you know?" when we self-satisfied youngsters made generalisations based on :"It's a well known fact, that ...." . We sensed, rather than clearly understood, that he was, as we would say today, "anti-Establishment".

He conveyed to us the overwhelming feeling of his generation against the horrors of the recent war - it had only finished a decade earlier, remember - and this must have raised questions in our young minds, questions of which the Establishment would certainly not have approved. He once read us the whole of Sherrif's anti-war play: *Journey's End* , with its deeply emotional emphasis on the futlity and sheer inhumanity of trench warfare. The crippling, unbearable effect it had on people's personality, is what left the deepest impression on me. The brutality of it all!

The class meetings enabled us to expand our own ability to express our feelings in public - and in front of a very critical public, at that. It's amazing how we learnt to cut each other down to size. Subjects for debate were seldom ostensibly political. Indeed, I do not believe

Wag was trying to politicise us, much less to propagandise us. He was determinedly independent and belonged to no political party. He would have abhorred the very word, propaganda. No, he was simply obeying his own impulses, probably not very clearly thought out, of openness to new ideas and dislike of the false and pretentious.

Another source of political stimulation was to be found on the Level, on Sunday mornings. Here was a veritable Hyde Park Corner on my own doorstep. It was different from what is there today. There was no children's playground and on weekdays it was deserted. But on Sundays there were platforms for speakers of many different kinds and from many different organisations. Some spoke from ground level, without the benefit of a platform. One of these was Harry Cowley, recently honoured with a biography published by QueenSpark Books. I am forced by honesty to recall that I regarded him as an old reactionary at the time, with his populist rhetoric and anti-socialist views. Maybe he changed after I left Brighton. Or maybe my perceptions were naive.

The platform speakers who always attracted me were those of the National Unemployed Workers' Movement. Their propaganda was crude but their meetings were lively.   They told of Hunger Marchers and their clashes with the police, painting a vivid picture of mounties charging starving men who had marched from the four corners of Britain to protest to the government against their treatment.

They proclaimed the right to a decent life for all - including those who were unemployed "through no fault of their own". One oft-repeated sarcastic joke was that as soon as an unemployed worker was seen enjoying a Woodbine (the cheapest cigarette at the time), this was taken as evidence that he was not entitled to his benefits. This was a reference to the Means Test, a method of refusing payment if the claimant was deemed to have resources of his own.

Here I cannot refrain from mentioning a family, father and three sons, black of hair and lively of eye, who brought their mandolins along and entertained us with revolutionary songs. They were the de Lacys; a foreign-sounding name but they were Brightonians to the core. The eldest son, Gus, was also a fiery speaker who could rouse the crowd with his oratory. By great good fortune, I caught up with Gus and one of his two brothers, Oscar, when I returned to Brighton some years after the war. They were both still full of fight and Gus still had his mandolin which, he told me, had accompanied him right through the war on his army service. Sadly, they have both died in the last few years.

Another character one used to see on the Level was a peculiar little man with a wide-brimmed, black felt hat and a heavy foreign accent, who used to sell The Daily Worker. I didn't buy one, I wasn't in the market for printed propaganda at that stage, but I connected the paper with the NUWM ever afterwards. Some of the most stimulating discussions and debates took place among those who had turned up to have a good Sunday morning argument. Those starting these impromptu discussions were usually people well versed in their subject and knew how to argue their case.

I gradually fell into the category of those around who wanted to challenge what was being said and express their standpoint. In this way, I sharpened my polemical skills and developed a confidence and, perhaps, a moral courage, which was to pitchfork me into that political struggle with which my life has been closely interwoven almost ever since. At the time, I was full of these arguments, both at school and, later, at work where I incautiously pursued them, sometimes arousing antipathy or derision. At any rate, these experiences made me feel part of something exciting, progressive, thought-provoking and - most important - with a future!

I was also aware, perhaps to a limited extent, of what was going on in the big wide world beyond Brighton's sunny clime. The NUWM speakers had made me feel the plight of the unemployed and a detestation of "the boss class" and its hated Means Test, making parents dependent on their children and tearing families apart. I knew that Ramsay Macdonald had "gone over to the other side" by joining a coalition with the Tories and some Liberals, for the purpose of forming a National Government in the emergency created by the slump, the mass unemployment which resulted from it and the demands of the financiers for tough measures to deal with the situation.

His Labour Government was temporarily superseded by a Lab/Cons/Lib coalition to form a "National" Government, though a small group, led by George Lansbury, remained true to the Labour Party. An election was called to broadcast the message:"We've all got to tighten our belts!" I recall a Labour poster which graphically summed up the answer to this doleful message. It was entitled: "Equality of sacrifice." It shows a brick wall with a ladder up against it. Flood water reaches halfway up the wall and covers the bottom part of the ladder. Three men stand on different rungs of the ladder. At the top is a top-hatted gentleman labelled, £1000 a year. Just below him stands a bowler-hatted man labelled, £500 a year, he is sufficiently low down for his feet to be getting wet. Lower still, and up to his neck in water, is a cloth-capped worker. And the caption reads: Man at the top: "Let's all take one step lower down the ladder!"

There was a great deal of heated debate but I noticed that most people accepted the argument that "the country" was in a bad way and we all had to unite and make sacrifices to fight the slump, just as we had united to fight the enemy during the war. Even my parents later admitted, rather shamefacedly, that they had voted "National".

I attended an election meeting which took place in the hall of my old school. I was accompanied by the boy upstairs, the one I had the occasional friendly fights with. We both looked forward to the excitement of political debate. It was a Labour Party meeting and one of their two candidates (Brighton was a double constituency) was speaking, supported by another speaker. There were about 30 or more people present.

Lewis Cohen, the candidate, was the main speaker and the other was the editor of Reynolds News, the weekly Co-op paper. He was a dour Scot and a complete contrast to the extrovert, bubbling Brightonian. This latter started off by citing a well known comedian who, with mock anxiety, would appeal to his audience with: "Giv's a chance, giv's a chance". The speaker obviously knew what he was up against. Sure enough whenever, in the middle of his oration, there was mild barracking, out came this despairing cry: "Giv's a chance, giv's a chance." I noted this, even at that early age, as a neat oratorical trick to get the audience on his side with a bit of humour. And he had just the manner to pull it off, ought perhaps to have been a music hall turn, himself.

One other incident I recall is meeting Mr. Landon, the Irishman who lived in our basement, just outside the house and as we passed the time of day he said, in his usual friendly way: "I suppose we're on two different sides of the fence, in this election". When I think of the acrimony that sometimes accompanies political comment these days, I am doubly appreciative of his attitude then. Incidentally, I didn't notice many political posters round our way and those I did see were all Conservative - or Unionist, as they called themselves then. The full name was Conservative and Unionist Party; nothing to do with trade unions, of course, but indicative of their connections with the Protestant group in Northern Ireland.

In Brighton, the result of the election was a foregone conclusion. The Tories obtained the highest majority any party has ever achieved in a British election before or since: Major Tryon and Sir Cooper Rawson, over 75,000 each and Lewis Cohen and his running mate, Mrs. Moore, under 13,000 !   Mrs.Moore was a candidate of the Co-operative Party, which is affiliated to the Labour Party and this may explain why the editor of Reynolds News was speaking at the public meeting I attended.

The Brighton result was simply an extreme example of what happened throughout the country. The Labour Party's vote was decimated and the "National" Government swept the board. The situation was depicted as so dire that only a "government of national unity" could hope to deal with the danger "threatening the nation". Indeed, I can remember reading the words of Philip Snowdon, who had also deserted the Labour Party and who, just incidentally, became the Chancellor of the Exchequer in the new government.

He described the policy of those remaining in the Labour Party as: "Bolshevism gone mad!" This comparison of the pale pink Labour Party with Lenin's revolutionary "party of a new type" in Russia may sound ludicrous today, but it gives a flavour of the whipped-up public sentiment which sent the Labour Party crashing to defeat. Maybe the situation could have been transformed if the Labour Party *had* been a bit more "Bolshevik".

GOODBYE BRIGHTON!

For some time, in the autumn of 1931, discussions were going on between my parents about the possibility - indeed the need - to leave Brighton and try our luck in London. Things had got to such a pass in my father's business affairs, that a change of tack was becoming urgent. I suppose they considered that London, the centre of the universe as far as we provincials were concerned, would offer better business prospects.

It seemed that the bank was unwilling to provide further loans on the house, as we already owed them its full worth! Around the turn of the year a great deal of our furniture was packed and sent off, presumably to be stored in London and we were confined to the large bedroom and the kitchen. A very cosy arrangement if rather cramped. We even entertained visitors there.

When my firm were told of our intentions they seemed very loth to let me go. My father went to see them to explain the situation. They offered to accommodate me in one of their properties, give me free board and lodgings and increase my salary, if I would stay. Although we were very tempted by this offer, it was decided to reject it. I probably had little influence on the decision but, even if I'd had more say, I think I'd have opted for the move.

The fact is, we children were thoroughly fed up with Brighton and the restrictions its provincialism placed upon us. I suppose it was a sort of progression, beginning from our earliest memories. First there was Weston, the sleepy, West-country seaside, with its semi-rural atmosphere and the great park which was our playground and an important part of our world.

Then breezy, cosmopolitan Brighton, a different sort of playground, at once larger, fresher, cheekier, somehow more adult which, from long acquaintance, had now become too crabbed and confined for our young yearnings and wing-spreading desires. We imagined that, somewhere out there, in the big wide world, there was adventure, excitemement, opportunity and all sorts of vaguely conceived delights. We had relatives of various sorts in London and a large circle of friends, only waiting to make our social lives more interesting.

There were, of course, many worries attached to the move, the financial one being the most depressing. When we finally left, the bank took the house as payment for the debt. My parents must have been more worried than we were, as they were more aware of the situation; arriving in a new town, with few resources and fewer prospects. How would we fare? How would we keep our heads above water? I'm sure father was full of apprehension although he didn't seem to show it outwardly. And some of this tension must have rubbed off on us.

Additionally, we were somewhat nervous, as one always is, about taking a new, decisive step into an unknown world. Along with our elation at the thought of the joys that awaited us, underneath we wondered how London would receive us. I know that I harboured a terrible inferiority complex about the small-town image I had of myself. I was ready to be offended at the thought that the Londoners would look down on us as country bumpkins and outsmart us at every turn.

All my experience from about five onwards had been in this unique seaside town. Its sights and sounds, its atmosphere, its whole ambience had entered into my adolescent soul. I felt I was a Brightonian through and through, with all its breezy image and coastal wisdom and perhaps its prejudices too. I was about to immerse myself in a different world and, young as I was, I felt the immense importance of this for my future life.

No doubt each member of the family had their own silent thoughts, as we boarded the coach that was to take us to our new life in the metropolis. I don't know what other passengers on that memorable journey were feeling but we children were certainly pent up with emotion. Clear in my mind, as though it were yesterday, is the sound of the cheer that we four sent up as we sped through the famous Brighton gates.

Our future was, as yet, unknown: the exciting, anxiety-ridden Thirties, with the dark, ever present shadow of unemployment; the wonderful, colourful friendships and social experiences; my political development and involvement; my fanatical support of the Arsenal (just around the corner from my home); the West End store (in Regent St.) where I worked for several years before moving on to a well paid traveller's job with Mars Confections, having first to learn to drive and then own a car (a Morris 8) but which ended when I was hospitalised with appendicitis; the great May Day demonstrations and the struggle for peace; the nightmare slide to war after Chamberlain's dastardly betrayal at Munich; my work in Birmingham; my army years, culminating in Burma and Malaya. I shall not go on. That cheer we sent up was a symbolic gesture: goodbye to the old way of life, goodbye childhood - goodbye Brighton!

Photograph by Grant and Vincent 1997.

The author was born in the Midlands, on August 7th 1916 but he lived with his family in Brighton from his early youth, spending his schooldays there. He started work in Brighton as a draper's assistant, soon after his fourteenth birthday. Some months before his sixteenth birthday, the family left for London where they enjoyed a very varied social life. He attended LCC Evening Classes in English, Maths and Shorthand, obtaining RSA Cetificates. At the same time he was reading voraciously, especially political and historical works. He worked first in a large drapery store in the West End and later for Mars Confections as a commercial traveller. He was in Coventry, working for his father when war broke out and in 1940 he was called up and served for 6 years, the last four in India and Burma.

On his return from abroad he came back to his parents who were living in Birmingham and enrolled in the Emergency Teacher Training Scheme. After an intensive eleven-month course he returned to London, where he taught for ten years, mainly in one of the earliest Comprehensive Schools and, after a 5-year evening course at LSE, obtained a BSc (Econ).

In 1958 he was offered a post as Lektor at the university in Leipzig and taught English there for seven years. It was in Leipzig that he met Rita Kühn whom he married in 1963. They returned to England two years later and Len took up a teaching post at Dorothy Stringer School in Brighton where he became Head of History. He retired from teaching in 1980 and has since been busy on a number of different projects and activities, of which the writing of this book was probably the most significant. He has a daughter and granddaughter and recently celebrated his eightieth birthday.